SELECTED WORKS

OF

RENE DESCARTES

Translated by John Veitch

Containing:

Discourse On The Method Of Rightly Conducting
The Reason, And Seeking Truth In The Sciences

Meditations On First Philosophy

Selections From The Principles Of Philosophy

DISCOURSE ON THE METHOD OF RIGHTLY CONDUCTING THE REASON, AND SEEKING TRUTH IN THE SCIENCES

by

Rene Descartes

Translated by John Veitch

PREFATORY NOTE BY THE AUTHOR

If this Discourse appear too long to be read at once, it may be divided into six Parts: and, in the first, will be found various considerations touching the Sciences; in the second, the principal rules of the Method which the Author has discovered, in the third, certain of the rules of Morals which he has deduced from this Method; in the fourth, the reasonings by which he establishes the existence of God and of the Human Soul, which are the foundations of his Metaphysic; in the fifth, the order of the Physical questions which he has investigated, and, in particular, the explication of the motion of the heart and of some other difficulties pertaining to Medicine, as also the difference between the soul of man and that of the brutes; and, in the last, what the Author believes to be required in order to greater advancement in the investigation of Nature than has yet been made, with the reasons that have induced him to write.

PART I

Good sense is, of all things among men, the most equally distributed; for every one thinks himself so abundantly provided with it, that those even who are the most difficult to satisfy in everything else, do not usually desire a larger measure of this quality than they already possess. And in this it is not likely that all are mistaken the conviction is rather to be held as testifying that the power of judging aright and of distinguishing truth from error, which is properly what is called good sense or reason, is by nature equal in all men; and that the diversity of our opinions, consequently, does not arise from some being endowed with a larger share of reason than others, but solely from this, that we conduct our thoughts along different ways, and do not fix our attention on the same objects. For to be possessed of a vigorous mind is not enough; the prime requisite is rightly to apply it. The greatest minds, as they are capable of the highest excellences, are open likewise to the greatest aberrations; and those who travel very slowly may yet make far greater progress, provided they keep always to the straight road, than those who, while they run, forsake it.

For myself, I have never fancied my mind to be in any respect more perfect than those of the generality; on the contrary, I have often wished that I were equal to some others in promptitude of thought, or in clearness and distinctness of imagination, or in fullness and readiness of memory. And besides these, I know of no other qualities that contribute to the perfection of the mind; for as to the reason or sense, inasmuch as it is that alone which constitutes us men, and distinguishes us from the brutes, I am disposed to believe that it is to be found complete in each individual; and on this point to adopt the common opinion of philosophers, who say that the difference of greater and less holds only among the accidents, and not among the forms or natures of individuals of the same species.

I will not hesitate, however, to avow my belief that it has been my singular good fortune to have very early in life fallen in with certain tracks which have conducted me to considerations and maxims, of which I have formed a method that gives me the means, as I think, of gradually augmenting my knowledge, and of raising it by little and little to the highest point which the mediocrity of my talents and the brief duration of my life will permit me to reach. For I have already reaped from it such fruits that, although I have been accustomed to think lowly enough of myself, and although when I look with the eye of a philosopher at the varied courses and pursuits of mankind at large, I find scarcely one which does not appear in vain and useless, I nevertheless derive the highest satisfaction from the progress I conceive myself to have already made in the search after truth, and cannot help entertaining such expectations of the future as to believe that if, among the occupations of men as men, there is any one really excellent and important, it is that which I have chosen.

After all, it is possible I may be mistaken; and it is but a little copper and glass, perhaps, that I take for gold and diamonds. I know how very liable we are to delusion in what relates to ourselves, and also how much the judgments of our friends are to be suspected when given in our favor. But I shall endeavor in this discourse to describe the paths I have followed, and to delineate my life as in a picture, in order that each one may also be able to judge of them for himself, and that in the general opinion entertained of them, as gathered from current report, I myself may have a new help towards instruction to be added to those I have been in the habit of employing.

My present design, then, is not to teach the method which each ought to follow for the right conduct of his reason, but solely to describe the way in which I have endeavored to conduct my own. They who set themselves to give precepts must of course regard themselves as possessed of greater skill than those to whom they prescribe; and if they err in the slightest particular, they subject themselves to censure. But as this tract is put forth merely as a history, or, if you will, as a tale, in which, amid some examples worthy of imitation, there will be found, perhaps, as many more which it were advisable not to follow, I hope it will prove useful to some without being hurtful to any, and that my openness will find some favor with all.

From my childhood, I have been familiar with letters; and as I was given to believe that by their help a clear and certain knowledge of all that is useful in life might be acquired, I was ardently desirous of instruction. But as soon as I had finished the entire course of study, at the close of which it is customary to be admitted into the order of the learned, I completely changed my opinion. For I found myself involved in so many doubts and errors, that I was convinced I had advanced no farther in all my attempts at learning, than the discovery at every turn of my own ignorance. And yet I was studying in one of the most celebrated schools in Europe, in which I thought there must be learned men, if such were anywhere to be found. I had been taught all that others learned there; and not contented with the sciences actually taught us, I had, in addition, read all the books that had fallen into my hands, treating of such branches as are esteemed the most curious and rare. I knew the judgment which others had formed of me; and I did not find that I was considered inferior to my fellows, although there were among them some who were already marked out to fill the places of our instructors. And, in fine, our age appeared to me as flourishing, and as fertile in powerful minds as any preceding one. I was thus led to take the liberty of judging of all other men by myself, and of concluding that there was no science in existence that was of such a nature as I had previously been given to believe.

I still continued, however, to hold in esteem the studies of the schools. I was aware that the languages taught in them are necessary to the understanding of the writings of the ancients; that the grace of fable stirs the mind; that the memorable deeds of history elevate it; and, if read with discretion, aid in forming the judgment; that the perusal of all excellent books is, as it were, to interview with the noblest men of past ages, who have written them, and even a studied interview, in which are discovered to us only their choicest thoughts; that eloquence has incomparable force and beauty; that poesy has its ravishing graces and delights;

that in the mathematics there are many refined discoveries eminently suited to gratify the inquisitive, as well as further all the arts an lessen the labour of man; that numerous highly useful precepts and exhortations to virtue are contained in treatises on morals; that theology points out the path to heaven; that philosophy affords the means of discoursing with an appearance of truth on all matters, and commands the admiration of the more simple; that jurisprudence, medicine, and the other sciences, secure for their cultivators honors and riches; and, in fine, that it is useful to bestow some attention upon all, even upon those abounding the most in superstition and error, that we may be in a position to determine their real value, and guard against being deceived.

But I believed that I had already given sufficient time to languages, and likewise to the reading of the writings of the ancients, to their histories and fables. For to hold converse with those of other ages and to travel, are almost the same thing. It is useful to know something of the manners of different nations, that we may be enabled to form a more correct judgment regarding our own, and be prevented from thinking that everything contrary to our customs is ridiculous and irrational, a conclusion usually come to by those whose experience has been limited to their own country. On the other hand, when too much time is occupied in traveling, we become strangers to our native country; and the over curious in the customs of the past are generally ignorant of those of the present. Besides, fictitious narratives lead us to imagine the possibility of many events that are impossible; and even the most faithful histories, if they do not wholly misrepresent matters, or exaggerate their importance to render the account of them more worthy of perusal, omit, at least, almost always the meanest and least striking of the attendant circumstances; hence it happens that the remainder does not represent the truth, and that such as regulate their conduct by examples drawn from this source, are apt to fall into the extravagances of the knight-errants of romance, and to entertain projects that exceed their powers.

I esteemed eloquence highly, and was in raptures with poesy; but I thought that both were gifts of nature rather than fruits of study. Those in whom the faculty of reason is predominant, and who most skillfully dispose their thoughts with a view to render them clear and intelligible, are always the best able to persuade others of the truth of what they lay down, though they should speak only in the language of Lower Brittany, and be wholly ignorant of the rules of rhetoric; and those whose minds are stored with the most agreeable fancies, and who can give expression to them with the greatest embellishment and harmony, are still the best poets, though unacquainted with the art of poetry.

I was especially delighted with the mathematics, on account of the certitude and evidence of their reasonings; but I had not as yet a precise knowledge of their true use; and thinking that they but contributed to the advancement of the mechanical arts, I was astonished that foundations, so strong and solid, should have had no loftier superstructure reared on them. On the other hand, I compared the disquisitions of the ancient moralists to very towering and magnificent palaces with no better foundation than sand and mud: they laud the virtues very highly, and exhibit them as estimable far above anything on earth; but they give us no adequate criterion of virtue, and frequently that which they designate with so fine a name is but apathy, or pride, or despair, or parricide.

I revered our theology, and aspired as much as any one to reach heaven: but being given assuredly to understand that the way is not less open to the most ignorant than to the most learned, and that the revealed truths which lead to heaven are above our comprehension, I did not presume to subject them to the impotency of my reason; and I thought that in order competently to undertake their examination, there was need of some special help from heaven, and of being more than man.

Of philosophy I will say nothing, except that when I saw that it had been cultivated for many ages by the most distinguished men, and that yet there is not a single matter within its sphere which is not still in dispute, and nothing, therefore, which is above doubt, I did not presume to anticipate that my success would be greater in it than that of others; and further, when I considered the number of conflicting opinions touching a single matter that may be upheld by learned men, while there can be but one true, I reckoned as well-nigh false all that was only probable.

As to the other sciences, inasmuch as these borrow their principles from philosophy, I judged that no solid superstructures could be reared on foundations so infirm; and neither the honor nor the gain held out by them was sufficient to determine me to their cultivation: for I was not, thank Heaven, in a condition which compelled me to make merchandise of science for the bettering of my fortune; and though I might not profess to scorn glory as a cynic, I yet made very slight account of that honor which I hoped to acquire only through fictitious titles. And, in fine, of false sciences I thought I knew the worth sufficiently to escape being deceived by the professions of an alchemist, the predictions of an astrologer, the impostures of a magician, or by the artifices and boasting of any of those who profess to know things of which they are ignorant.

For these reasons, as soon as my age permitted me to pass from under the control of my instructors, I entirely abandoned the study of letters, and resolved no longer to seek any other science than the knowledge of myself, or of the great book of the world. I spent the remainder of my youth in traveling, in visiting courts and armies, in holding intercourse with men of different dispositions and ranks, in collecting varied experience, in proving myself in the different situations into which fortune threw me, and, above all, in making such reflection on the matter of my experience as to secure my improvement. For it occurred to me that I should find much more truth in the reasonings of each individual with reference to the affairs in which he is personally interested, and the issue of which must presently punish him if he has judged amiss, than in those conducted by a man of letters in his study, regarding speculative matters that are of no practical moment, and followed by no consequences to himself, farther, perhaps, than that they foster his vanity the better the more remote they are from common sense; requiring, as they must in this case, the exercise of greater ingenuity and art to render them probable. In addition, I had always a most earnest desire to know how to distinguish the true from the false, in order that I might be able clearly to discriminate the right path in life, and proceed in it with confidence.

It is true that, while busied only in considering the manners of other men, I found here, too, scarce any ground for settled conviction, and remarked hardly less contradiction among them than in the opinions of the philosophers. So that the greatest advantage I derived from the study consisted in this, that, observing many things which, however extravagant and ridiculous to our apprehension, are yet by common consent received and approved by other great nations, I learned to entertain too decided a belief in regard to nothing of the truth of which I had been persuaded merely by example and custom; and thus I gradually extricated myself from many errors powerful enough to darken our natural intelligence, and incapacitate us in great measure from listening to reason. But after I had been occupied several years in thus studying the book of the world, and in essaying to gather some experience, I at length resolved to make myself an object of study, and to employ all the powers of my mind in choosing the paths I ought to follow, an undertaking which was accompanied with greater success than it would have been had I never quitted my country or my books.

PART II

I was then in Germany, attracted thither by the wars in that country, which have not yet been brought to a termination; and as I was returning to the army from the coronation of the emperor, the setting in of winter arrested me in a locality where, as I found no society to interest me, and was besides fortunately undisturbed by any cares or passions, I remained the whole day in seclusion, with full opportunity to occupy my attention with my own thoughts. Of these one of the very first that occurred to me was, that there is seldom so much perfection in works composed of many separate parts, upon which different hands had been employed, as in those completed by a single master. Thus it is observable that the buildings which a single architect has planned and executed, are generally more elegant and commodious than those which several have attempted to improve, by making old walls serve for purposes for which they were not originally built. Thus also, those ancient cities which, from being at first only villages, have become, in course of time, large towns, are usually but ill laid out compared with the regularity constructed towns which a professional architect has freely planned on an open plain; so that although the several buildings of the former may often equal or surpass in beauty those of the latter, yet when one observes their indiscriminate juxtaposition, there a large one and here a small, and the consequent crookedness and irregularity of the streets, one is disposed to allege that chance rather than any human will guided by reason must have led to such an arrangement. And if we consider that nevertheless there have been at all times certain officers whose duty it was to see that private buildings contributed to public ornament, the difficulty of reaching high perfection with but the materials of others to operate on, will be readily acknowledged. In the same way I fancied that those nations which, starting from a semi-barbarous state and advancing to civilization by slow degrees, have had their laws successively determined, and, as it were, forced upon them simply by experience of the hurtfulness of particular crimes and disputes, would by this process come to be possessed of less perfect institutions than those which, from the commencement of their association as communities, have followed the appointments of some wise legislator. It is thus quite certain that the constitution of the true religion, the ordinances of which are derived from God, must be incomparably superior to that of every other. And, to speak of human affairs, I believe that the pre-eminence of Sparta was due not to the goodness of each of its laws in particular, for many of these were very strange, and even opposed to good morals, but to the circumstance that, originated by a single individual, they all tended to a single end. In the same way I thought that the sciences contained in books (such of them at least as are made up of probable reasonings, without demonstrations), composed as they are of the opinions of many different individuals massed together, are farther removed from truth than the simple inferences which a man of good sense using his natural and unprejudiced judgment draws respecting the matters of his experience. And because we have all to pass through a state of infancy to manhood, and have been of necessity, for a length of time, governed by our desires and preceptors (whose dictates were frequently conflicting, while neither perhaps always counseled us for the best), I farther concluded that it is almost impossible that our judgments can be so correct or solid as they would have been, had our reason been mature from the moment of our birth, and had we always been guided by it alone.

It is true, however, that it is not customary to pull down all the houses of a town with the single design of rebuilding them differently, and thereby rendering the streets more handsome; but it often happens that a private individual takes down his own with the view of erecting it anew, and that people are even sometimes constrained to this when their houses are in danger of falling from age, or when the foundations are insecure. With this before me by way of example, I was persuaded that it would indeed be preposterous for a private individual to think of reforming a state by fundamentally changing it throughout, and overturning it in order to set it up amended; and the same I thought was true of any similar project for reforming the body of the sciences, or the order of teaching them established in the schools: but as for the opinions which up to that time I had embraced, I thought that I could not do better than resolve at once to sweep them wholly away, that I might afterwards be in a position to admit either others more correct, or even perhaps the same when they had undergone the scrutiny of reason. I firmly believed that in this way I should much better succeed in the conduct of my life, than if I built only upon old foundations, and leaned upon principles which, in my youth, I had taken upon trust. For although I recognized various difficulties in this undertaking, these were not, however, without remedy, nor once to be compared with such as attend the slightest reformation in public affairs. Large bodies, if once overthrown, are with great difficulty set up again, or even kept erect when once seriously shaken, and the fall of such is always disastrous. Then if there are any imperfections in the constitutions of states (and that many such exist the diversity of constitutions is alone sufficient to assure us), custom has without doubt materially smoothed their inconveniences, and has even managed to steer altogether clear of, or insensibly corrected a number which sagacity could not have provided against with equal effect; and, in fine, the defects are almost always more tolerable than the change necessary for their removal; in the same manner that highways which wind among mountains, by being much frequented, become gradually so smooth and commodious, that it is much better to follow them than to seek a straighter path by climbing over the tops of rocks and descending to the bottoms of precipices.

Hence it is that I cannot in any degree approve of those restless and busy meddlers who, called neither by birth nor fortune to take part in the management of public affairs, are yet always projecting reforms; and if I thought that this tract contained aught which might justify the suspicion that I was a victim of such folly, I would by no means permit its publication. I have never contemplated anything higher than the reformation of my own opinions, and basing them on a foundation wholly my own. And although my own satisfaction with my work has led me to present here a draft of it, I do not by any means therefore recommend to every one else to make a similar attempt. Those whom God has endowed with a larger measure of genius will entertain, perhaps, designs still more exalted; but for the many I am much afraid lest even the present undertaking be more than they can safely venture to imitate. The single design to strip one's self of all past beliefs is one that ought not to be taken by every one. The majority of men is composed of two classes, for neither of which would this be at all a befitting resolution: in the first place, of those who with more than a due confidence in their own powers, are precipitate in their judgments and want the patience requisite for orderly and circumspect thinking; whence it happens, that if men of this class once take the liberty to doubt of their accustomed opinions, and quit the beaten highway, they will never be able to thread the byway that would lead them by a shorter course, and will lose themselves and continue to wander for life; in the second place, of those who, possessed of sufficient sense or modesty to determine that there are others who excel them in the power of discriminating between truth and error, and by whom they may be instructed, ought rather to content themselves with the opinions of such than trust for more correct to their own reason.

For my own part, I should doubtless have belonged to the latter class, had I received instruction from but one master, or had I never known the diversities of opinion that from time immemorial have prevailed among men of the greatest learning. But I had become aware, even so early as during my college life, that no opinion, however absurd and incredible, can be imagined, which has not been maintained by some on of the philosophers; and afterwards in the course of my travels I remarked that all those whose opinions are decidedly repugnant to ours are not in that account barbarians and savages, but on the contrary that many of these nations make an equally good, if not better, use of their reason than we do. I took into account also the very different character which a person brought up from infancy in France or Germany exhibits, from that which, with the same mind originally, this individual would have possessed had he lived always among the Chinese or with savages, and the circumstance that in dress itself the fashion which pleased us ten years ago, and which may again, perhaps, be received into favor before ten years have gone, appears to us at this moment extravagant and ridiculous. I was thus led to infer that the ground of our opinions is far more custom and example than any certain knowledge. And, finally, although such be the ground of our opinions, I remarked that a plurality of suffrages is no guarantee of truth where it is at all of difficult discovery, as in such cases it is much more likely that it will be found by one than by many. I could, however, select from the crowd no one whose opinions seemed worthy of preference, and thus I found myself constrained, as it were, to use my own reason in the conduct of my life.

But like one walking alone and in the dark, I resolved to proceed so slowly and with such circumspection, that if I did not advance far, I would at least guard against falling. I did not even choose to dismiss summarily any of the opinions that had crept into my belief without having been introduced by reason, but first of all took sufficient time carefully to satisfy myself of the general nature of the task I was setting myself, and ascertain the true method by which to arrive at the knowledge of whatever lay within the compass of my powers.

Among the branches of philosophy, I had, at an earlier period, given some attention to logic, and among those of the mathematics to geometrical analysis and algebra,--three arts or sciences which ought, as I conceived, to contribute something to my design. But, on examination, I found that, as for logic, its syllogisms and the majority of its other precepts are of avail-- rather in the communication of what we already know, or even as the art of Lully, in speaking without judgment of things of which we are ignorant, than in the investigation of the unknown; and although this science contains indeed a number of correct and very excellent precepts, there are, nevertheless, so many others, and these either injurious or superfluous, mingled with the former, that it is almost quite as difficult to effect a severance of the true from the false as it is to extract a Diana or a Minerva from a rough block of marble. Then as to the analysis of the ancients and the algebra of the moderns, besides that they embrace only matters highly abstract, and, to appearance, of no use, the former is so exclusively restricted to the consideration of figures, that it can exercise the understanding only on condition of greatly fatiguing the imagination; and, in the latter, there is so complete a subjection to certain rules and formulas, that there results an art full of confusion and obscurity calculated to embarrass, instead of a science fitted to cultivate the mind. By these considerations I was induced to seek some other method which would comprise the advantages of the three and be exempt from their defects. And as a multitude of laws often only hampers justice, so that a state is best governed when, with few laws, these are rigidly administered; in like manner, instead of the great number of precepts of which logic is composed, I believed that the four following would prove perfectly sufficient for me, provided I took the firm and unwavering resolution never in a single instance to fail in observing them.

The first was never to accept anything for true which I did not clearly know to be such; that is to say, carefully to avoid precipitancy and prejudice, and to comprise nothing more in my judgement than what was presented to my mind so clearly and distinctly as to exclude all ground of doubt.

The second, to divide each of the difficulties under examination into as many parts as possible, and as might be necessary for its adequate solution.

The third, to conduct my thoughts in such order that, by commencing with objects the simplest and easiest to know, I might ascend by little and little, and, as it were, step by step, to the knowledge of the more complex; assigning in thought a certain order even to those objects which in their own nature do not stand in a relation of antecedence and sequence.

And the last, in every case to make enumerations so complete, and reviews so general, that I might be assured that nothing was omitted.

The long chains of simple and easy reasonings by means of which geometers are accustomed to reach the conclusions of their most difficult demonstrations, had led me to imagine that all things, to the knowledge of which man is competent, are mutually connected in the same way, and that there is nothing so far removed from us as to be beyond our reach, or so hidden that we cannot discover it, provided only we abstain from accepting the false for the true, and always preserve in our thoughts the order necessary for the deduction of one truth from another. And I had little difficulty in determining the objects with which it was necessary to commence, for I was already persuaded that it must be with the simplest and easiest to know, and, considering that of all those who have hitherto sought truth in the sciences, the mathematicians alone have been able to find any demonstrations, that is, any certain and evident reasons, I did not doubt but that such must have been the rule of their investigations. I resolved to commence, therefore, with the examination of the simplest objects, not anticipating, however, from this any other advantage than that to be found in accustoming my mind to the love and nourishment of truth, and to a distaste for all such reasonings as were unsound. But I had no intention on that account of attempting to master all the particular sciences commonly denominated mathematics: but observing that, however different their objects, they all agree in considering only the various relations or proportions subsisting among those objects, I thought it best for my purpose to consider these proportions in the most general form possible, without referring them to any objects in particular, except such as would most facilitate the knowledge of them, and without by any means restricting them to these, that afterwards I might thus be the better able to apply them to every other class of objects to which they are legitimately applicable. Perceiving further, that in order to understand these relations I should sometimes have to consider them one by one and sometimes only to bear them in mind, or embrace them in the aggregate, I thought that, in order the better to consider them individually, I should view them as subsisting between straight lines, than which I could find no objects more simple, or capable of being more distinctly represented to my imagination and senses; and on the other hand, that in order to retain them in the memory or embrace an aggregate of many, I should express them by certain characters the briefest possible. In this way I believed that I could borrow all that was best both in geometrical analysis and in algebra, and correct all the defects of the one by help of the other.

And, in point of fact, the accurate observance of these few precepts gave me, I take the liberty of saying, such ease in unraveling all the questions embraced in these two sciences, that in the two or three months I devoted to their examination, not only did I reach solutions of questions I had formerly deemed exceedingly difficult but even as regards questions of the solution of which I continued ignorant, I was enabled, as it appeared to me, to determine the means whereby, and the extent to which a solution was possible; results attributable to the circumstance that I commenced with the simplest and most general truths, and that thus each truth discovered was a rule available in the discovery of subsequent ones Nor in this perhaps shall I appear too vain, if it be considered that, as the truth on any particular point is one whoever apprehends the truth, knows all that on that point can be known. The child, for example, who has been instructed in the elements of arithmetic, and has made a particular addition, according to rule, may be assured that he has found, with respect to the sum of the numbers before him, and that in this instance is within the reach of human genius. Now, in conclusion, the method which teaches adherence to the true order, and an exact enumeration of all the conditions of the thing sought includes all that gives certitude to the rules of arithmetic.

But the chief ground of my satisfaction with thus method, was the assurance I had of thereby exercising my reason in all matters, if not with absolute perfection, at least with the greatest attainable by me: besides, I was conscious that by its use my mind was becoming gradually habituated to clearer and more distinct conceptions of its objects; and I hoped also, from not having restricted this method to any particular matter, to apply it to the difficulties of the other sciences, with not less success than to those of algebra. I should not, however, on this account have ventured at once on the examination of all the difficulties of the sciences which presented themselves to me, for this would have been contrary to the order prescribed in the method, but observing that the knowledge of such is dependent on principles borrowed from philosophy, in which I found nothing certain, I thought it necessary first of all to endeavor to establish its principles. And because I observed, besides, that an inquiry of this kind was of all others of the greatest moment, and one in which precipitancy and anticipation in judgment were most to be dreaded, I thought that I ought not to approach it till I had reached a more mature age (being at that time but twenty-three), and had first of all employed much of my time in preparation for the work, as well by eradicating from my mind all the erroneous opinions I had up to that moment accepted, as by amassing variety of experience to afford materials for my reasonings, and by continually exercising myself in my chosen method with a view to increased skill in its application.

PART III

And finally, as it is not enough, before commencing to rebuild the house in which we live, that it be pulled down, and materials and builders provided, or that we engage in the work ourselves, according to a plan which we have beforehand carefully drawn out, but as it is likewise necessary that we be furnished with some other house in which we may live commodiously during the operations, so that I might not remain irresolute in my actions, while my reason compelled me to suspend my judgement, and that I might not be prevented from living thenceforward in the greatest possible felicity, I formed a provisory code of morals, composed of three or four maxims, with which I am desirous to make you acquainted.

The first was to obey the laws and customs of my country, adhering firmly to the faith in which, by the grace of God, I had been educated from my childhood and regulating my conduct in every other matter according to the most moderate opinions, and the farthest removed from extremes, which should happen to be adopted in practice with general consent of the most judicious of those among whom I might be living. For as I had from that time begun to hold my own opinions for nought because I wished to subject them all to examination, I was convinced that I could not do better than follow in the meantime the opinions of the most judicious; and although there are some perhaps among the Persians and Chinese as judicious as among ourselves, expediency seemed to dictate that I should regulate my practice conformably to the opinions of those with whom I should have to live; and it appeared to me that, in order to ascertain the real opinions of such, I ought rather to take cognizance of what they practised than of what they said, not only because, in the corruption of our manners, there are few disposed to speak exactly as they believe, but also because very many are not aware of what it is that they really believe; for, as the act of mind by which a thing is believed is different from that by which we know that we believe it, the one act is often found without the other. Also, amid many opinions held in equal repute, I chose always the most moderate, as much for the reason that these are always the most convenient for practice, and probably the best (for all excess is generally vicious), as that, in the event of my falling into error, I might be at less distance from the truth than if, having chosen one of the extremes, it should turn out to be the other which I ought to have adopted. And I placed in the class of extremes especially all promises by which somewhat of our freedom is abridged; not that I disapproved of the laws which, to provide against the instability of men of feeble resolution, when what is sought to be accomplished is some good, permit engagements by vows and contracts binding the parties to persevere in it, or even, for the security of commerce, sanction similar engagements where the purpose sought to be realized is indifferent: but because I did not find anything on earth which was wholly superior to change, and because, for myself in particular, I hoped gradually to perfect my judgments, and not to suffer them to deteriorate, I would have deemed it a grave sin against good sense, if, for the reason that I approved of something at a particular time, I therefore bound myself to hold it for good at a subsequent time, when perhaps it had ceased to be so, or I had ceased to esteem it such.

My second maxim was to be as firm and resolute in my actions as I was able, and not to adhere less steadfastly to the most doubtful opinions, when once adopted, than if they had been highly certain; imitating in this the example of travelers who, when they have lost their way in a forest, ought not to wander from side to side, far less remain in one place, but proceed constantly towards the same side in as straight a line as possible, without changing their direction for slight reasons, although perhaps it might be chance alone which at first determined the selection; for in this way, if they do not exactly reach the point they desire, they will come at least in the end to some place that will probably be preferable to the middle of a forest. In the same way, since in action it frequently happens that no delay is permissible, it is very certain that, when it is not in our power to determine what is true, we ought to act according to what is most probable; and even although we should not remark a greater probability in one opinion than in another, we ought notwithstanding to choose one or the other, and afterwards consider it, in so far as it relates to practice, as no longer dubious, but manifestly true and certain, since the reason by which our choice has been determined is itself possessed of these qualities. This principle was sufficient thenceforward to rid me of all those repentings and pangs of remorse that usually disturb the consciences of such feeble and uncertain minds as, destitute of any clear and determinate principle of choice, allow themselves one day to adopt a course of action as the best, which they abandon the next, as the opposite.

My third maxim was to endeavor always to conquer myself rather than fortune, and change my desires rather than the order of the world, and in general, accustom myself to the persuasion that, except our own thoughts, there is nothing absolutely in our power; so that when we have done our best in things external to us, all wherein we fail of success is to be held, as regards us, absolutely impossible: and this single principle seemed to me sufficient to prevent me from desiring for the future anything which I could not obtain, and thus render me contented; for since our will naturally seeks those objects alone which the understanding represents as in some way possible of attainment, it is plain, that if we consider all external goods as equally beyond our power, we shall no more regret the absence of such goods as seem due to our birth, when deprived of them without any fault of ours, than our not possessing the kingdoms of China or Mexico, and thus making, so to speak, a virtue of necessity, we shall no more desire health in disease, or freedom in imprisonment, than we now do bodies incorruptible as diamonds, or the wings of birds to fly with. But I confess there is need of prolonged discipline and frequently repeated meditation to accustom the mind to view all objects in this light; and I believe that in this chiefly consisted the secret of the power of such philosophers as in former times were enabled to rise superior to the influence of fortune, and, amid suffering and poverty, enjoy a happiness which their gods might have envied. For, occupied incessantly with the consideration of the limits prescribed to their power by nature, they became so entirely convinced that nothing was at their disposal except their own thoughts, that this conviction was of itself sufficient to prevent their entertaining any desire of other objects; and over their thoughts they acquired a sway so absolute, that they had some ground on this account for esteeming themselves more rich and more powerful, more free and more happy, than other men who, whatever be the favors heaped on them by nature and fortune, if destitute of this philosophy, can never command the realization of all their desires.

In fine, to conclude this code of morals, I thought of reviewing the different occupations of men in this life, with the view of making choice of the best. And, without wishing to offer any remarks on the employments of others, I may state that it was my conviction that I could not do better than continue in that in which I was engaged, viz., in devoting my whole life to the culture of my reason, and in making the greatest progress I was able in the knowledge of truth, on the principles of the method which I had prescribed to myself. This method, from the time I had begun to apply it, had been to me the source of satisfaction so intense as to lead me to, believe that more perfect or more innocent could not be enjoyed in this life; and as by its means I daily discovered truths that appeared to me of some importance, and of which other men were generally ignorant, the gratification thence arising so occupied my mind that I was wholly indifferent to every other object. Besides, the three preceding maxims were founded singly on the design of continuing the work of self-instruction. For since God has endowed each of us with some light of reason by which to distinguish truth from error, I could not have believed that I ought for a single moment to rest satisfied with the opinions of another, unless I had resolved to exercise my own judgment in examining these whenever I should be duly qualified for the task. Nor could I have proceeded on such opinions without scruple, had I supposed that I should thereby forfeit any advantage for attaining still more accurate, should such exist. And, in fine, I could not have restrained my desires, nor remained satisfied had I not followed a path in which I thought myself certain of attaining all the knowledge to the acquisition of which I was competent, as well as the largest amount of what is truly good which I could ever hope to secure Inasmuch as we neither seek nor shun any object except in so far as our understanding represents it as good or bad, all that is necessary to right action is right judgment, and to the best action the most correct judgment, that is, to the acquisition of all the virtues with all else that is truly valuable and within our reach; and the assurance of such an acquisition cannot fail to render us contented.

Having thus provided myself with these maxims, and having placed them in reserve along with the truths of faith, which have ever occupied the first place in my belief, I came to the conclusion that I might with freedom set about ridding myself of what remained of my opinions. And, inasmuch as I hoped to be better able successfully to accomplish this work by holding intercourse with mankind, than by remaining longer shut up in the retirement where these thoughts had occurred to me, I betook me again to traveling before the winter was well ended. And, during the nine subsequent years, I did nothing but roam from one place to another, desirous of being a spectator rather than an actor in the plays exhibited on the theater of the world; and, as I made it my business in each matter to reflect particularly upon what might fairly be doubted and prove a source of error, I gradually rooted out from my mind all the errors which had hitherto crept into it. Not that in this I imitated the sceptics who doubt only that they may doubt, and seek nothing beyond uncertainty itself; for, on the contrary, my design was singly to find ground of assurance, and cast aside the loose earth and sand, that I might reach the rock or the clay. In this, as appears to me, I was successful enough; for, since I endeavored to discover the falsehood or incertitude of the propositions I examined, not by feeble conjectures, but by clear and certain reasonings, I met with nothing so doubtful as not to yield some conclusion of adequate certainty, although this were merely the inference, that the matter in question contained nothing certain. And, just as in pulling down an old house, we usually reserve the ruins to contribute towards the erection, so, in destroying such of my opinions as I judged to be Ill-founded, I made a variety of observations and acquired an amount of experience of which I availed myself in the establishment of more certain. And further, I continued to exercise myself in the method I had prescribed; for, besides taking care in general to conduct all my thoughts according to its rules, I reserved some hours from time to time which I expressly devoted to the employment of the method in the solution of mathematical difficulties, or even in the solution likewise of some questions belonging to other sciences, but which, by my having detached them from such principles of these sciences as were of inadequate certainty, were rendered almost mathematical: the truth of this will be manifest from the numerous examples contained in this volume. And thus, without in appearance living otherwise than those who, with no other occupation than that of spending their lives agreeably and innocently, study to sever pleasure from vice, and who, that they may enjoy their leisure without ennui, have recourse to such pursuits as are honorable, I was nevertheless prosecuting my design, and making greater progress in the knowledge of truth, than I might, perhaps, have made had I been engaged in the perusal of books merely, or in holding converse with men of letters.

These nine years passed away, however, before I had come to any determinate judgment respecting the difficulties which form matter of dispute among the learned, or had commenced to seek the principles of any philosophy more certain than the vulgar. And the examples of many men of the highest genius, who had, in former times, engaged in this inquiry, but, as appeared to me, without success, led me to imagine it to be a work of so much difficulty, that I would not perhaps have ventured on it so soon had I not heard it currently rumored that I had already completed the inquiry. I know not what were the grounds of this opinion; and, if my conversation contributed in any measure to its rise, this must have happened rather from my having confessed my Ignorance with greater freedom than those are accustomed to do who have studied a little, and expounded perhaps, the reasons that led me to doubt of many of those things that by others are esteemed certain, than from my having boasted of any system of philosophy. But, as I am of a disposition that makes me unwilling to be esteemed different from what I really am, I thought it necessary to endeavor by all means to render myself worthy of the reputation accorded to me; and it is now exactly eight years since this desire constrained me to remove from all those places where interruption from any of my acquaintances was possible, and betake myself to this country, in which the long duration of the war has led to the establishment of such discipline, that the armies maintained seem to be of use only in enabling the inhabitants to enjoy more securely the blessings of peace and where, in the midst of a great crowd actively engaged in business, and more careful of their own affairs than curious about those of others, I have been enabled to live without being deprived of any of the conveniences to be had in the most populous cities, and yet as solitary and as retired as in the midst of the most remote deserts.

PART IV

I am in doubt as to the propriety of making my first meditations in the place above mentioned matter of discourse; for these are so metaphysical, and so uncommon, as not, perhaps, to be acceptable to every one. And yet, that it may be determined whether the foundations that I have laid are sufficiently secure, I find myself in a measure constrained to advert to them. I had long before remarked that, in relation to practice, it is sometimes necessary to adopt, as if above doubt, opinions which we discern to be highly uncertain, as has been already said; but as I then desired to give my attention solely to the search after truth, I thought that a procedure exactly the opposite was called for, and that I ought to reject as absolutely false all opinions in regard to which I could suppose the least ground for doubt, in order to ascertain whether after that there remained aught in my belief that was wholly indubitable. Accordingly, seeing that our senses sometimes deceive us, I was willing to suppose that there existed nothing really such as they presented to us; and because some men err in reasoning, and fall into paralogisms, even on the simplest matters of geometry, I, convinced that I was as open to error as any other, rejected as false all the reasonings I had hitherto taken for demonstrations; and finally, when I considered that the very same thoughts (presentations) which we experience when awake may also be experienced when we are asleep, while there is at that time not one of them true, I supposed that all the objects (presentations) that had ever entered into my mind when awake, had in them no more truth than the illusions of my dreams. But immediately upon this I observed that, whilst I thus wished to think that all was false, it was absolutely necessary that I, who thus thought, should be somewhat; and as I observed that this truth, I think, therefore I am (COGITO ERGO SUM), was so certain and of such evidence that no ground of doubt, however extravagant, could be alleged by the sceptics capable of shaking it, I concluded that I might, without scruple, accept it as the first principle of the philosophy of which I was in search.

In the next place, I attentively examined what I was and as I observed that I could suppose that I had no body, and that there was no world nor any place in which I might be; but that I could not therefore suppose that I was not; and that, on the contrary, from the very circumstance that I thought to doubt of the truth of other things, it most clearly and certainly followed that I was; while, on the other hand, if I had only ceased to think, although all the other objects which I had ever imagined had been in reality existent, I would have had no reason to believe that I existed; I thence concluded that I was a substance whose whole essence or nature consists only in thinking, and which, that it may exist, has need of no place, nor is dependent on any material thing; so that "I," that is to say, the mind by which I am what I am, is wholly distinct from the body, and is even more easily known than the latter, and is such, that although the latter were not, it would still continue to be all that it is.

After this I inquired in general into what is essential I to the truth and certainty of a proposition; for since I had discovered one which I knew to be true, I thought that I must likewise be able to discover the ground of this certitude. And as I observed that in the words I think, therefore I am, there is nothing at all which gives me assurance of their truth beyond this, that I see very clearly that in order to think it is necessary to exist, I concluded that I might take, as a general rule, the principle, that all the things which we very clearly and distinctly conceive are true, only observing, however, that there is some difficulty in rightly determining the objects which we distinctly conceive.

In the next place, from reflecting on the circumstance that I doubted, and that consequently my being was not wholly perfect (for I clearly saw that it was a greater perfection to know than to doubt), I was led to inquire whence I had learned to think of something more perfect than myself; and I clearly recognized that I must hold this notion from some nature which in reality was more perfect. As for the thoughts of many other objects external to me, as of the sky, the earth, light, heat, and a thousand more, I was less at a loss to know whence these came; for since I remarked in them nothing which seemed to render them superior to myself, I could believe that, if these were true, they were dependencies on my own nature, in so far as it possessed a certain perfection, and, if they were false, that I held them from nothing, that is to say, that they were in me because of a certain imperfection of my nature. But this could not be the case with-the idea of a nature more perfect than myself; for to receive it from nothing was a thing manifestly impossible; and, because it is not less repugnant that the more perfect should be an effect of, and dependence on the less perfect, than that something should proceed from nothing, it was equally impossible that I could hold it from myself: accordingly, it but remained that it had been placed in me by a nature which was in reality more perfect than mine, and which even possessed within itself all the perfections of which I could form any idea; that is to say, in a single word, which was God. And to this I added that, since I knew some perfections which I did not possess, I was not the only being in existence (I will here, with your permission, freely use the terms of the schools); but, on the contrary, that there was of necessity some other more perfect Being upon whom I was dependent, and from whom I had received all that I possessed; for if I had existed alone, and independently of every other being, so as to have had from myself all the perfection, however little, which I actually possessed, I should have been able, for the same reason, to have had from myself the whole remainder of perfection, of the want of which I was conscious, and thus could of myself have become infinite, eternal, immutable, omniscient, all-powerful, and, in fine, have possessed all the perfections which I could recognize in God. For in order to know the nature of God (whose existence has been established by the preceding reasonings), as far as my own nature permitted, I had only to consider in reference to all the properties of which I found in my mind some idea, whether their possession was a mark of perfection; and I was assured that no one which indicated any imperfection was in him, and that none of the rest was awanting. Thus I perceived that doubt, inconstancy, sadness, and such like, could not be found in God, since I myself would have been happy to be free from them. Besides, I had ideas of many sensible and corporeal things; for although I might suppose that I was dreaming, and that all which I saw or imagined was false, I could not, nevertheless, deny that the ideas were in reality in my thoughts. But, because I had already very clearly recognized in myself that the intelligent nature is distinct from the corporeal, and as I observed that all composition is an evidence of dependency, and that a state of dependency is manifestly a state of imperfection, I therefore determined that it could not be a perfection in God to be compounded of these two natures and that consequently he was not so compounded; but that if there were any bodies in the world, or even any intelligences, or other natures that were not wholly perfect, their existence depended on his power in such a way that they could not subsist without him for a single moment.

I was disposed straightway to search for other truths and when I had represented to myself the object of the geometers, which I conceived to be a continuous body or a space indefinitely extended in length, breadth, and height or depth, divisible into divers parts which admit of different figures and sizes, and of being moved or transposed in all manner of ways (for all this the geometers suppose to be in the object they contemplate), I went over some of their simplest demonstrations. And, in the first place, I observed, that the great certitude which by common consent is accorded to these demonstrations, is founded solely upon this, that they are clearly conceived in accordance with the rules I have already laid down In the next place, I perceived that there was nothing at all in these demonstrations which could assure me of the existence of their object: thus, for example, supposing a triangle to be given, I distinctly perceived that its three angles were necessarily equal to two right angles, but I did not on that account perceive anything which could assure me that any triangle existed: while, on the contrary, recurring to the examination of the idea of a Perfect Being, I found that the existence of the Being was comprised in the idea in the same way that the equality of its three angles to two right angles is comprised in the idea of a triangle, or as in the idea of a sphere, the equidistance of all points on its surface from the center, or even still more clearly; and that consequently it is at least as certain that God, who is this Perfect Being, is, or exists, as any demonstration of geometry can be.

But the reason which leads many to persuade them selves that there is a difficulty in knowing this truth, and even also in knowing what their mind really is, is that they never raise their thoughts above sensible objects, and are so accustomed to consider nothing except by way of imagination, which is a mode of thinking limited to material objects, that all that is not imaginable seems to them not intelligible. The truth of this is sufficiently manifest from the single circumstance, that the philosophers of the schools accept as a maxim that there is nothing in the understanding which was not previously in the senses, in which however it is certain that the ideas of God and of the soul have never been; and it appears to me that they who make use of their imagination to comprehend these ideas do exactly the some thing as if, in order to hear sounds or smell odors, they strove to avail themselves of their eyes; unless indeed that there is this difference, that the sense of sight does not afford us an inferior assurance to those of smell or hearing; in place of which, neither our imagination nor our senses can give us assurance of anything unless our understanding intervene.

Finally, if there be still persons who are not sufficiently persuaded of the existence of God and of the soul, by the reasons I have adduced, I am desirous that they should know that all the other propositions, of the truth of which they deem themselves perhaps more assured, as that we have a body, and that there exist stars and an earth, and such like, are less certain; for, although we have a moral assurance of these things, which is so strong that there is an appearance of extravagance in doubting of their existence, yet at the same time no one, unless his intellect is impaired, can deny, when the question relates to a metaphysical certitude, that there is sufficient reason to exclude entire assurance, in the observation that when asleep we can in the same way imagine ourselves possessed of another body and that we see other stars and another earth, when there is nothing of the kind. For how do we know that the thoughts which occur in dreaming are false rather than those other which we experience when awake, since the former are often not less vivid and distinct than the latter? And though men of the highest genius study this question as long as they please, I do not believe that they will be able to give any reason which can be sufficient to remove this doubt, unless they presuppose the existence of God. For, in the first place even the principle which I have already taken as a rule, viz., that all the things which we clearly and distinctly conceive are true, is certain only because God is or exists and because he is a Perfect Being, and because all that we possess is derived from him: whence it follows that our ideas or notions, which to the extent of their clearness and distinctness are real, and proceed from God, must to that extent be true. Accordingly, whereas we not infrequently have ideas or notions in which some falsity is contained, this can only be the case with such as are to some extent confused and obscure, and in this proceed from nothing (participate of negation), that is, exist in us thus confused because we are not wholly perfect. And it is evident that it is not less repugnant that falsity or imperfection, in so far as it is imperfection, should proceed from God, than that truth or perfection should proceed from nothing. But if we did not know that all which we possess of real and true proceeds from a Perfect and Infinite Being, however clear and distinct our ideas might be, we should have no ground on that account for the assurance that they possessed the perfection of being true.

But after the knowledge of God and of the soul has rendered us certain of this rule, we can easily understand that the truth of the thoughts we experience when awake, ought not in the slightest degree to be called in question on account of the illusions of our dreams. For if it happened that an individual, even when asleep, had some very distinct idea, as, for example, if a geometer should discover some new demonstration, the circumstance of his being asleep would not militate against its truth; and as for the most ordinary error of our dreams, which consists in their representing to us various objects in the same way as our external senses, this is not prejudicial, since it leads us very properly to suspect the truth of the ideas of sense; for we are not infrequently deceived in the same manner when awake; as when persons in the jaundice see all objects yellow, or when the stars or bodies at a great distance appear to us much smaller than they are. For, in fine, whether awake or asleep, we ought never to allow ourselves to be persuaded of the truth of anything unless on the evidence of our reason. And it must be noted that I say of our reason, and not of our imagination or of our senses: thus, for example, although we very clearly see the sun, we ought not therefore to determine that it is only of the size which our sense of sight presents; and we may very distinctly imagine the head of a lion joined to the body of a goat, without being therefore shut up to the conclusion that a chimaera exists; for it is not a dictate of reason that what we thus see or imagine is in reality existent; but it plainly tells us that all our ideas or notions contain in them some truth; for otherwise it could not be that God, who is wholly perfect and veracious, should have placed them in us. And because our reasonings are never so clear or so complete during sleep as when we are awake, although sometimes the acts of our imagination are then as lively and distinct, if not more so than in our waking moments, reason further dictates that, since all our thoughts cannot be true because of our partial imperfection, those possessing truth must infallibly be found in the experience of our waking moments rather than in that of our dreams.

PART V

I would here willingly have proceeded to exhibit the whole chain of truths which I deduced from these primary but as with a view to this it would have been necessary now to treat of many questions in dispute among the earned, with whom I do not wish to be embroiled, I believe that it will be better for me to refrain from this exposition, and only mention in general what these truths are, that the more judicious may be able to determine whether a more special account of them would conduce to the public advantage. I have ever remained firm in my original resolution to suppose no other principle than that of which I have recently availed myself in demonstrating the existence of God and of the soul, and to accept as true nothing that did not appear to me more clear and certain than the demonstrations of the geometers had formerly appeared; and yet I venture to state that not only have I found means to satisfy myself in a short time on all the principal difficulties which are usually treated of in philosophy, but I have also observed certain laws established in nature by God in such a manner, and of which he has impressed on our minds such notions, that after we have reflected sufficiently upon these, we cannot doubt that they are accurately observed in all that exists or takes place in the world and farther, by considering the concatenation of these laws, it appears to me that I have discovered many truths more useful and more important than all I had before learned, or even had expected to learn.

But because I have essayed to expound the chief of these discoveries in a treatise which certain considerations prevent me from publishing, I cannot make the results known more conveniently than by here giving a summary of the contents of this treatise. It was my design to comprise in it all that, before I set myself to write it, I thought I knew of the nature of material objects. But like the painters who, finding themselves unable to represent equally well on a plain surface all the different faces of a solid body, select one of the chief, on which alone they make the light fall, and throwing the rest into the shade, allow them to appear only in so far as they can be seen while looking at the principal one; so, fearing lest I should not be able to compense in my discourse all that was in my mind, I resolved to expound singly, though at considerable length, my opinions regarding light; then to take the opportunity of adding something on the sun and the fixed stars, since light almost wholly proceeds from them; on the heavens since they transmit it; on the planets, comets, and earth, since they reflect it; and particularly on all the bodies that are upon the earth, since they are either colored, or transparent, or luminous; and finally on man, since he is the spectator of these objects. Further, to enable me to cast this variety of subjects somewhat into the shade, and to express my judgment regarding them with greater freedom, without being necessitated to adopt or refute the opinions of the learned, I resolved to leave all the people here to their disputes, and to speak only of what would happen in a new world, if God were now to create somewhere in the imaginary spaces matter sufficient to compose one, and were to agitate variously and confusedly the different parts of this matter, so that there resulted a chaos as disordered as the poets ever feigned, and after that did nothing more than lend his ordinary concurrence to nature, and allow her to act in accordance with the laws which he had established. On this supposition, I, in the first place, described this matter, and essayed to represent it in such a manner that to my mind there can be nothing clearer and more intelligible, except what has been recently said regarding God and the soul; for I even expressly supposed that it possessed none of those forms or qualities which are so debated in the schools, nor in general anything the knowledge of which is not so natural to our minds that no one can so much as imagine himself ignorant of it. Besides, I have pointed out what are the laws of nature; and, with no other principle upon which to found my reasonings except the infinite perfection of God, I endeavored to demonstrate all those about which there could be any room for doubt, and to prove that they are such, that even if God had created more worlds, there could have been none in which these laws were not observed. Thereafter, I showed how the greatest part of the matter of this chaos must, in accordance with these laws, dispose and arrange itself in such a way as to present the appearance of heavens; how in the meantime some of its parts must compose an earth and some planets and comets, and others a sun and fixed stars. And, making a digression at this stage on the subject of light, I expounded at considerable length what the nature of that light must be which is found in the sun and the stars, and how thence in an instant of time it traverses the immense spaces of the heavens, and how from the planets and comets it is reflected towards the earth. To this I likewise added much respecting the substance, the situation, the motions, and all the different qualities of these heavens and stars; so that I thought I had said enough respecting them to show that there is nothing observable in the heavens or stars of our system that must not, or at least may not appear precisely alike in those of the system which I described. I came next to speak of the earth in particular, and to show how, even though I had expressly supposed that God had given no weight to the matter of which it is composed, this should not prevent all its parts from tending exactly to its center; how with water and air on its surface, the disposition of the heavens and heavenly bodies, more especially of the moon, must cause a flow and ebb, like in all its circumstances to that observed in our seas, as also a certain current both of water and air from east to west, such as is likewise observed between the tropics; how the mountains, seas, fountains, and rivers might naturally be formed in it, and the metals produced in the mines, and the plants grow in the fields and in general, how all the bodies which are commonly denominated mixed or composite might be generated and, among other things in the discoveries alluded to inasmuch as besides the stars, I knew nothing except fire which produces light, I spared no pains to set forth all that pertains to its nature,--the manner of its production and support, and to explain how heat is sometimes found without light, and light without heat; to show how it can induce various colors upon different bodies and other diverse qualities; how it reduces some to a liquid state and hardens others; how it can consume almost all bodies, or convert them into ashes and smoke; and finally, how from these ashes, by the mere intensity of its action, it forms glass: for as this transmutation of ashes into glass appeared to me as wonderful as any other in nature, I took a special pleasure in describing it. I was not, however, disposed, from these circumstances, to conclude that this world had been created in the manner I described; for it is much more likely that God made it at the first such as it was to be. But this is certain, and an opinion commonly received among theologians, that the action by which he now sustains it is the same with that by which he originally created it; so that even although he had from the beginning given it no other form than that of chaos, provided only he had established certain laws of nature, and had lent it his concurrence to enable it to act as it is wont to do, it may be believed, without discredit to the miracle of creation, that, in this way alone, things purely material might, in course of time, have become such as we observe them at present; and their nature is much more easily conceived when they are beheld coming in this manner gradually into existence, than when they are only considered as produced at once in a finished and perfect state.

From the description of inanimate bodies and plants, I passed to animals, and particularly to man. But since I had not as yet sufficient knowledge to enable me to treat of these in the same manner as of the rest, that is to say, by deducing effects from their causes, and by showing from what elements and in what manner nature must produce them, I remained satisfied with the supposition that God formed the body of man wholly like to one of ours, as well in the external shape of the members as in the internal conformation of the organs, of the same matter with that I had described, and at first placed in it no rational soul, nor any other principle, in room of the vegetative or sensitive soul, beyond kindling in the heart one of those fires without light, such as I had already described, and which I thought was not different from the heat in hay that has been heaped together before it is dry, or that which causes fermentation in new wines before they are run clear of the fruit. For, when I examined the kind of functions which might, as consequences of this supposition, exist in this body, I found precisely all those which may exist in us independently of all power of thinking, and consequently without being in any measure owing to the soul; in other words, to that part of us which is distinct from the body, and of which it has been said above that the nature distinctively consists in thinking, functions in which the animals void of reason may be said wholly to resemble us; but among which I could not discover any of those that, as dependent on thought alone, belong to us as men, while, on the other hand, I did afterwards discover these as soon as I supposed God to have created a rational soul, and to have annexed it to this body in a particular manner which I described.

But, in order to show how I there handled this matter, I mean here to give the explication of the motion of the heart and arteries, which, as the first and most general motion observed in animals, will afford the means of readily determining what should be thought of all the rest. And that there may be less difficulty in understanding what I am about to say on this subject, I advise those who are not versed in anatomy, before they commence the perusal of these observations, to take the trouble of getting dissected in their presence the heart of some large animal possessed of lungs (for this is throughout sufficiently like the human), and to have shown to them its two ventricles or cavities: in the first place, that in the right side, with which correspond two very ample tubes, viz., the hollow vein (vena cava), which is the principal receptacle of the blood, and the trunk of the tree, as it were, of which all the other veins in the body are branches; and the arterial vein (vena arteriosa), inappropriately so denominated, since it is in truth only an artery, which, taking its rise in the heart, is divided, after passing out from it, into many branches which presently disperse themselves all over the lungs; in the second place, the cavity in the left side, with which correspond in the same manner two canals in size equal to or larger than the preceding, viz., the venous artery (arteria venosa), likewise inappropriately thus designated, because it is simply a vein which comes from the lungs, where it is divided into many branches, interlaced with those of the arterial vein, and those of the tube called the windpipe, through which the air we breathe enters; and the great artery which, issuing from the heart, sends its branches all over the body. I should wish also that such persons were carefully shown the eleven pellicles which, like so many small valves, open and shut the four orifices that are in these two cavities, viz., three at the entrance of the hollow veins where they are disposed in such a manner as by no means to prevent the blood which it contains from flowing into the right ventricle of the heart, and yet exactly to prevent its flowing out; three at the entrance to the arterial vein, which, arranged in a manner exactly the opposite of the former, readily permit the blood contained in this cavity to pass into the lungs, but hinder that contained in the lungs from returning to this cavity; and, in like manner, two others at the mouth of the venous artery, which allow the blood from the lungs to flow into the left cavity of the heart, but preclude its return; and three at the mouth of the great artery, which suffer the blood to flow from the heart, but prevent its reflux. Nor do we need to seek any other reason for the number of these pellicles beyond this that the orifice of the venous artery being of an oval shape from the nature of its situation, can be adequately closed with two, whereas the others being round are more conveniently closed with three. Besides, I wish such persons to observe that the grand artery and the arterial vein are of much harder and firmer texture than the venous artery and the hollow vein; and that the two last expand before entering the heart, and there form, as it were, two pouches denominated the auricles of the heart, which are composed of a substance similar to that of the heart itself; and that there is always more warmth in the heart than in any other part of the body--and finally, that this heat is capable of causing any drop of blood that passes into the cavities rapidly to expand and dilate, just as all liquors do when allowed to fall drop by drop into a highly heated vessel.

For, after these things, it is not necessary for me to say anything more with a view to explain the motion of the heart, except that when its cavities are not full of blood, into these the blood of necessity flows,--from the hollow vein into the right, and from the venous artery into the left; because these two vessels are always full of blood, and their orifices, which are turned towards the heart, cannot then be closed. But as soon as two drops of blood have thus passed, one into each of the cavities, these drops which cannot but be very large, because the orifices through which they pass are wide, and the vessels from which they come full of blood, are immediately rarefied, and dilated by the heat they meet with. In this way they cause the whole heart to expand, and at the same time press home and shut the five small valves that are at the entrances of the two vessels from which they flow, and thus prevent any more blood from coming down into the heart, and becoming more and more rarefied, they push open the six small valves that are in the orifices of the other two vessels, through which they pass out, causing in this way all the branches of the arterial vein and of the grand artery to expand almost simultaneously with the heart which immediately thereafter begins to contract, as do also the arteries, because the blood that has entered them has cooled, and the six small valves close, and the five of the hollow vein and of the venous artery open anew and allow a passage to other two drops of blood, which cause the heart and the arteries again to expand as before. And, because the blood which thus enters into the heart passes through these two pouches called auricles, it thence happens that their motion is the contrary of that of the heart, and that when it expands they contract. But lest those who are ignorant of the force of mathematical demonstrations and who are not accustomed to distinguish true reasons from mere verisimilitudes, should venture, without examination, to deny what has been said, I wish it to be considered that the motion which I have now explained follows as necessarily from the very arrangement of the parts, which may be observed in the heart by the eye alone, and from the heat which may be felt with the fingers, and from the nature of the blood as learned from experience, as does the motion of a clock from the power, the situation, and shape of its counterweights and wheels.

But if it be asked how it happens that the blood in the veins, flowing in this way continually into the heart, is not exhausted, and why the arteries do not become too full, since all the blood which passes through the heart flows into them, I need only mention in reply what has been written by a physician of England, who has the honor of having broken the ice on this subject, and of having been the first to teach that there are many small passages at the extremities of the arteries, through which the blood received by them from the heart passes into the small branches of the veins, whence it again returns to the heart; so that its course amounts precisely to a perpetual circulation. Of this we have abundant proof in the ordinary experience of surgeons, who, by binding the arm with a tie of moderate straitness above the part where they open the vein, cause the blood to flow more copiously than it would have done without any ligature; whereas quite the contrary would happen were they to bind it below; that is, between the hand and the opening, or were to make the ligature above the opening very tight. For it is manifest that the tie, moderately straightened, while adequate to hinder the blood already in the arm from returning towards the heart by the veins, cannot on that account prevent new blood from coming forward through the arteries, because these are situated below the veins, and their coverings, from their greater consistency, are more difficult to compress; and also that the blood which comes from the heart tends to pass through them to the hand with greater force than it does to return from the hand to the heart through the veins. And since the latter current escapes from the arm by the opening made in one of the veins, there must of necessity be certain passages below the ligature, that is, towards the extremities of the arm through which it can come thither from the arteries. This physician likewise abundantly establishes what he has advanced respecting the motion of the blood, from the existence of certain pellicles, so disposed in various places along the course of the veins, in the manner of small valves, as not to permit the blood to pass from the middle of the body towards the extremities, but only to return from the extremities to the heart;

and farther, from experience which shows that all the blood which is in the body may flow out of it in a very short time through a single artery that has been cut, even although this had been closely tied in the immediate neighborhood of the heart and cut between the heart and the ligature, so as to prevent the supposition that the blood flowing out of it could come from any other quarter than the heart.

But there are many other circumstances which evince that what I have alleged is the true cause of the motion of the blood: thus, in the first place, the difference that is observed between the blood which flows from the veins, and that from the arteries, can only arise from this, that being rarefied, and, as it were, distilled by passing through the heart, it is thinner, and more vivid, and warmer immediately after leaving the heart, in other words, when in the arteries, than it was a short time before passing into either, in other words, when it was in the veins; and if attention be given, it will be found that this difference is very marked only in the neighborhood of the heart; and is not so evident in parts more remote from it. In the next place, the consistency of the coats of which the arterial vein and the great artery are composed, sufficiently shows that the blood is impelled against them with more force than against the veins. And why should the left cavity of the heart and the great artery be wider and larger than the right cavity and the arterial vein, were it not that the blood of the venous artery, having only been in the lungs after it has passed through the heart, is thinner, and rarefies more readily, and in a higher degree, than the blood which proceeds immediately from the hollow vein? And what can physicians conjecture from feeling the pulse unless they know that according as the blood changes its nature it can be rarefied by the warmth of the heart, in a higher or lower degree, and more or less quickly than before? And if it be inquired how this heat is communicated to the other members, must it not be admitted that this is effected by means of the blood, which, passing through the heart, is there heated anew, and thence diffused over all the body? Whence it happens, that if the blood be withdrawn from any part, the heat is likewise withdrawn by the same means; and although the heart were as-hot as glowing iron, it would not be capable of warming the feet and hands as at present, unless it continually sent thither new blood. We likewise perceive from this, that the true use of respiration is to bring sufficient fresh air into the lungs, to cause the blood which flows into them from the right ventricle of the heart, where it has been rarefied and, as it were, changed into vapors, to become thick, and to convert it anew into blood, before it flows into the left cavity, without which process it would be unfit for the nourishment of the fire that is there. This receives confirmation from the circumstance, that it is observed of animals destitute of lungs that they have also but one cavity in the heart, and that in children who cannot use them while in the womb, there is a hole through which the blood flows from the hollow vein into the left cavity of the heart, and a tube through which it passes from the arterial vein into the grand artery without passing through the lung. In the next place, how could digestion be carried on in the stomach unless the heart communicated heat to it through the arteries, and along with this certain of the more fluid parts of the blood, which assist in the dissolution of the food that has been taken in? Is not also the operation which converts the juice of food into blood easily comprehended, when it is considered that it is distilled by passing and repassing through the heart perhaps more than one or two hundred times in a day? And what more need be adduced to explain nutrition, and the production of the different humors of the body, beyond saying, that the force with which the blood, in being rarefied, passes from the heart towards the extremities of the arteries, causes certain of its parts to remain in the members at which they arrive, and there occupy the place of some others expelled by them; and that according to the situation, shape, or smallness of the pores with which they meet, some rather than others flow into certain parts, in the same way that some sieves are observed to act, which, by being variously perforated, serve to separate different species of grain? And, in the last place, what above all is here worthy of observation, is the generation of the animal spirits, which are like a very subtle wind, or rather a very pure and vivid flame which, continually ascending in great abundance from the heart to the brain, thence penetrates through the nerves into the muscles, and gives motion to all the members; so that to account for other parts of the blood which, as most agitated and penetrating, are the fittest to compose these spirits, proceeding towards the brain, it is not necessary to suppose any other cause, than simply, that the arteries which carry them thither proceed from the heart in the most direct lines, and that, according to the rules of mechanics which are the same with those of nature, when many objects tend at once to the same point where there is not sufficient room for all (as is the case with the parts of the blood which flow forth from the left cavity of the heart and tend towards the brain), the weaker and less agitated parts must necessarily be driven aside from that point by the stronger which alone in this way reach it I had expounded all these matters with sufficient minuteness in the treatise which I formerly thought of publishing. And after these, I had shown what must be the fabric of the nerves and muscles of the human body to give the animal spirits contained in it the power to move the members, as when we see heads shortly after they have been struck off still move and bite the earth, although no longer animated; what changes must take place in the brain to produce waking, sleep, and dreams; how light, sounds, odors, tastes, heat, and all the other qualities of external objects impress it with different ideas by means of the senses; how hunger, thirst, and the other internal affections can likewise impress upon it divers ideas; what must be understood by the common sense (sensus communis) in which these ideas are received, by the memory which retains them, by the fantasy which can change them in various ways, and out of them compose new ideas, and which, by the same means, distributing the animal spirits through the muscles, can cause the members of such a body to move in as many different ways, and in a manner as suited, whether to the objects that are presented to its senses or to its internal affections, as can take place in our own case apart from the guidance of the will. Nor will this appear at all strange to those who are acquainted with the variety of movements performed by the different automata, or moving machines fabricated by human industry, and that with help of but few pieces compared with the great multitude of bones, muscles, nerves, arteries, veins, and other parts that are found in the body of each animal. Such persons will look upon this body as a machine made by the hands of God, which is incomparably better arranged, and adequate to movements more admirable than is any machine of human invention. And here I specially stayed to show that, were there such machines exactly resembling organs and outward form an ape or any other irrational animal, we could have no means of knowing that they were in any respect of a different nature from these animals; but if there were machines bearing the image of our bodies, and capable of imitating our actions as far as it is morally possible, there would still remain two most certain tests whereby to know that they were not therefore really men. Of these the first is that they could never use words or other signs arranged in such a manner as is competent to us in order to declare our thoughts to others: for we may easily conceive a machine to be so constructed that it emits vocables, and even that it emits some correspondent to the action upon it of external objects which cause a change in its organs; for example, if touched in a particular place it may demand what we wish to say to it; if in another it may cry out that it is hurt, and such like; but not that it should arrange them variously so as appositely to reply to what is said in its presence, as men of the lowest grade of intellect can do. The second test is, that although such machines might execute many things with equal or perhaps greater perfection than any of us, they would, without doubt, fail in certain others from which it could be discovered that they did not act from knowledge, but solely from the disposition of their organs: for while reason is an universal instrument that is alike available on every occasion, these organs, on the contrary, need a particular arrangement for each particular action; whence it must be morally impossible that there should exist in any machine a diversity of organs sufficient to enable it to act in all the occurrences of life, in the way in which our reason enables us to act. Again, by means of these two tests we may likewise know the difference between men and brutes. For it is highly deserving of remark, that there are no men so dull and stupid, not even idiots, as to be incapable of joining together different words, and thereby constructing a declaration by which to make their thoughts understood; and that on the other hand, there is no other animal, however perfect or happily circumstanced, which can do the like. Nor does this inability arise from want of organs: for we observe that magpies and parrots can utter words like ourselves, and are yet unable to speak as we do, that is, so as to show that they understand what they say; in place of which men born deaf and dumb, and thus not less, but rather more than the brutes, destitute of the organs which others use in speaking, are in the habit of spontaneously inventing certain signs by which they discover their thoughts to those who, being usually in their company, have leisure to learn their language. And this proves not only that the brutes have less reason than man, but that they have none at all: for we see that very little is required to enable a person to speak; and since a certain inequality of capacity is observable among animals of the same species, as well as among men, and since some are more capable of being instructed than others, it is incredible that the most perfect ape or parrot of its species, should not in this be equal to the most stupid infant of its kind or at least to one that was crack-brained, unless the soul of brutes were of a nature wholly different from ours. And we ought not to confound speech with the natural movements which indicate the passions, and can be imitated by machines as well as manifested by animals; nor must it be thought with certain of the ancients, that the brutes speak, although we do not understand their language. For if such were the case, since they are endowed with many organs analogous to ours, they could as easily communicate their thoughts to us as to their fellows. It is also very worthy of remark, that, though there are many animals which manifest more industry than we in certain of their actions, the same animals are yet observed to show none at all in many others: so that the circumstance that they do better than we does not prove that they are endowed with mind, for it would thence follow that they possessed greater reason than any of us, and could surpass us in all things; on the contrary, it rather proves that they are destitute of reason, and that it is nature which acts in them according to the disposition of their organs: thus it is seen, that a clock composed only of wheels and weights can number the hours and measure time more exactly than we with all our skin.

I had after this described the reasonable soul, and shown that it could by no means be educed from the power of matter, as the other things of which I had spoken, but that it must be expressly created; and that it is not sufficient that it be lodged in the human body exactly like a pilot in a ship, unless perhaps to move its members, but that it is necessary for it to be joined and united more closely to the body, in order to have sensations and appetites similar to ours, and thus constitute a real man. I here entered, in conclusion, upon the subject of the soul at considerable length, because it is of the greatest moment: for after the error of those who deny the existence of God, an error which I think I have already sufficiently refuted, there is none that is more powerful in leading feeble minds astray from the straight path of virtue than the supposition that the soul of the brutes is of the same nature with our own; and consequently that after this life we have nothing to hope for or fear, more than flies and ants; in place of which, when we know how far they differ we much better comprehend the reasons which establish that the soul is of a nature wholly independent of the body, and that consequently it is not liable to die with the latter and, finally, because no other causes are observed capable of destroying it, we are naturally led thence to judge that it is immortal.

PART VI

Three years have now elapsed since I finished the treatise containing all these matters; and I was beginning to revise it, with the view to put it into the hands of a printer, when I learned that persons to whom I greatly defer, and whose authority over my actions is hardly less influential than is my own reason over my thoughts, had condemned a certain doctrine in physics, published a short time previously by another individual to which I will not say that I adhered, but only that, previously to their censure I had observed in it nothing which I could imagine to be prejudicial either to religion or to the state, and nothing therefore which would have prevented me from giving expression to it in writing, if reason had persuaded me of its truth; and this led me to fear lest among my own doctrines likewise some one might be found in which I had departed from the truth, notwithstanding the great care I have always taken not to accord belief to new opinions of which I had not the most certain demonstrations, and not to give expression to aught that might tend to the hurt of any one. This has been sufficient to make me alter my purpose of publishing them; for although the reasons by which I had been induced to take this resolution were very strong, yet my inclination, which has always been hostile to writing books, enabled me immediately to discover other considerations sufficient to excuse me for not undertaking the task. And these reasons, on one side and the other, are such, that not only is it in some measure my interest here to state them, but that of the public, perhaps, to know them.

I have never made much account of what has proceeded from my own mind; and so long as I gathered no other advantage from the method I employ beyond satisfying myself on some difficulties belonging to the speculative sciences, or endeavoring to regulate my actions according to the principles it taught me, I never thought myself bound to publish anything respecting it. For in what regards manners, every one is so full of his own wisdom, that there might be found as many reformers as heads, if any were allowed to take upon themselves the task of mending them, except those whom God has constituted the supreme rulers of his people or to whom he has given sufficient grace and zeal to be prophets; and although my speculations greatly pleased myself, I believed that others had theirs, which perhaps pleased them still more. But as soon as I had acquired some general notions respecting physics, and beginning to make trial of them in various particular difficulties, had observed how far they can carry us, and how much they differ from the principles that have been employed up to the present time, I believed that I could not keep them concealed without sinning grievously against the law by which we are bound to promote, as far as in us lies, the general good of mankind. For by them I perceived it to be possible to arrive at knowledge highly useful in life; and in room of the speculative philosophy usually taught in the schools, to discover a practical, by means of which, knowing the force and action of fire, water, air the stars, the heavens, and all the other bodies that surround us, as distinctly as we know the various crafts of our artisans, we might also apply them in the same way to all the uses to which they are adapted, and thus render ourselves the lords and possessors of nature. And this is a result to be desired, not only in order to the invention of an infinity of arts, by which we might be enabled to enjoy without any trouble the fruits of the earth, and all its comforts, but also and especially for the preservation of health, which is without doubt, of all the blessings of this life, the first and fundamental one; for the mind is so intimately dependent upon the condition and relation of the organs of the body, that if any means can ever be found to render men wiser and more ingenious than hitherto, I believe that it is in medicine they must be sought for. It is true that the science of medicine, as it now exists, contains few things whose utility is very remarkable: but without any wish to depreciate it, I am confident that there is no one, even among those whose profession it is, who does not admit that all at present known in it is almost nothing in comparison of what remains to be discovered; and that we could free ourselves from an infinity of maladies of body as well as of mind, and perhaps also even from the debility of age, if we had sufficiently ample knowledge of their causes, and of all the remedies provided for us by nature. But since I designed to employ my whole life in the search after so necessary a science, and since I had fallen in with a path which seems to me such, that if any one follow it he must inevitably reach the end desired, unless he be hindered either by the shortness of life or the want of experiments, I judged that there could be no more effectual provision against these two impediments than if I were faithfully to communicate to the public all the little I might myself have found, and incite men of superior genius to strive to proceed farther, by contributing, each according to his inclination and ability, to the experiments which it would be necessary to make, and also by informing the public of all they might discover, so that, by the last beginning where those before them had left off, and thus connecting the lives and labours of many, we might collectively proceed much farther than each by himself could do.

I remarked, moreover, with respect to experiments, that they become always more necessary the more one is advanced in knowledge; for, at the commencement, it is better to make use only of what is spontaneously presented to our senses, and of which we cannot remain ignorant, provided we bestow on it any reflection, however slight, than to concern ourselves about more uncommon and recondite phenomena: the reason of which is, that the more uncommon often only mislead us so long as the causes of the more ordinary are still unknown; and the circumstances upon which they depend are almost always so special and minute as to be highly difficult to detect. But in this I have adopted the following order: first, I have essayed to find in general the principles, or first causes of all that is or can be in the world, without taking into consideration for this end anything but God himself who has created it, and without educing them from any other source than from certain germs of truths naturally existing in our minds In the second place, I examined what were the first and most ordinary effects that could be deduced from these causes; and it appears to me that, in this way, I have found heavens, stars, an earth, and even on the earth water, air, fire, minerals, and some other things of this kind, which of all others are the most common and simple, and hence the easiest to know. Afterwards when I wished to descend to the more particular, so many diverse objects presented themselves to me, that I believed it to be impossible for the human mind to distinguish the forms or species of bodies that are upon the earth, from an infinity of others which might have been, if it had pleased God to place them there, or consequently to apply them to our use, unless we rise to causes through their effects, and avail ourselves of many particular experiments. Thereupon, turning over in my mind I the objects that had ever been presented to my senses I freely venture to state that I have never observed any which I could not satisfactorily explain by the principles had discovered. But it is necessary also to confess that the power of nature is so ample and vast, and these principles so simple and general, that I have hardly observed a single particular effect which I cannot at once recognize as capable of being deduced in man different modes from the principles, and that my greatest difficulty usually is to discover in which of these modes the effect is dependent upon them; for out of this difficulty cannot otherwise extricate myself than by again seeking certain experiments, which may be such that their result is not the same, if it is in the one of these modes at we must explain it, as it would be if it were to be explained in the other. As to what remains, I am now in a position to discern, as I think, with sufficient clearness what course must be taken to make the majority those experiments which may conduce to this end: but I perceive likewise that they are such and so numerous, that neither my hands nor my income, though it were a thousand times larger than it is, would be sufficient for them all; so that according as henceforward I shall have the means of making more or fewer experiments, I shall in the same proportion make greater or less progress in the knowledge of nature. This was what I had hoped to make known by the treatise I had written, and so clearly to exhibit the advantage that would thence accrue to the public, as to induce all who have the common good of man at heart, that is, all who are virtuous in truth, and not merely in appearance, or according to opinion, as well to communicate to me the experiments they had already made, as to assist me in those that remain to be made.

But since that time other reasons have occurred to me, by which I have been led to change my opinion, and to think that I ought indeed to go on committing to writing all the results which I deemed of any moment, as soon as I should have tested their truth, and to bestow the same care upon them as I would have done had it been my design to publish them. This course commended itself to me, as well because I thus afforded myself more ample inducement to examine them thoroughly, for doubtless that is always more narrowly scrutinized which we believe will be read by many, than that which is written merely for our private use (and frequently what has seemed to me true when I first conceived it, has appeared false when I have set about committing it to writing), as because I thus lost no opportunity of advancing the interests of the public, as far as in me lay, and since thus likewise, if my writings possess any value, those into whose hands they may fall after my death may be able to put them to what use they deem proper. But I resolved by no means to consent to their publication during my lifetime, lest either the oppositions or the controversies to which they might give rise, or even the reputation, such as it might be, which they would acquire for me, should be any occasion of my losing the time that I had set apart for my own improvement. For though it be true that every one is bound to promote to the extent of his ability the good of others, and that to be useful to no one is really to be worthless, yet it is likewise true that our cares ought to extend beyond the present, and it is good to omit doing what might perhaps bring some profit to the living, when we have in view the accomplishment of other ends that will be of much greater advantage to posterity. And in truth, I am quite willing it should be known that the little I have hitherto learned is almost nothing in comparison with that of which I am ignorant, and to the knowledge of which I do not despair of being able to attain; for it is much the same with those who gradually discover truth in the sciences, as with those who when growing rich find less difficulty in making great acquisitions, than they formerly experienced when poor in making acquisitions of much smaller amount. Or they may be compared to the commanders of armies, whose forces usually increase in proportion to their victories, and who need greater prudence to keep together the residue of their troops after a defeat than after a victory to take towns and provinces. For he truly engages in battle who endeavors to surmount all the difficulties and errors which prevent him from reaching the knowledge of truth, and he is overcome in fight who admits a false opinion touching a matter of any generality and importance, and he requires thereafter much more skill to recover his former position than to make great advances when once in possession of thoroughly ascertained principles. As for myself, if I have succeeded in discovering any truths in the sciences (and I trust that what is contained in this volume I will show that I have found some), I can declare that they are but the consequences and results of five or six principal difficulties which I have surmounted, and my encounters with which I reckoned as battles in which victory declared for me. I will not hesitate even to avow my belief that nothing further is wanting to enable me fully to realize my designs than to gain two or three similar victories; and that I am not so far advanced in years but that, according to the ordinary course of nature, I may still have sufficient leisure for this end. But I conceive myself the more bound to husband the time that remains the greater my expectation of being able to employ it aright, and I should doubtless have much to rob me of it, were I to publish the principles of my physics: for although they are almost all so evident that to assent to them no more is needed than simply to understand them, and although there is not one of them of which I do not expect to be able to give demonstration, yet, as it is impossible that they can be in accordance with all the diverse opinions of others, I foresee that I should frequently be turned aside from my grand design, on occasion of the opposition which they would be sure to awaken.

It may be said, that these oppositions would be useful both in making me aware of my errors, and, if my speculations contain anything of value, in bringing others to a fuller understanding of it; and still farther, as many can see better than one, in leading others who are now beginning to avail themselves of my principles, to assist me in turn with their discoveries. But though I recognize my extreme liability to error, and scarce ever trust to the first thoughts which occur to me, yet the experience I have had of possible objections to my views prevents me from anticipating any profit from them. For I have already had frequent proof of the judgments, as well of those I esteemed friends, as of some others to whom I thought I was an object of indifference, and even of some whose malignancy and envy would, I knew, determine them to endeavor to discover what partiality concealed from the eyes of my friends. But it has rarely happened that anything has been objected to me which I had myself altogether overlooked, unless it were something far removed from the subject: so that I have never met with a single critic of my opinions who did not appear to me either less rigorous or less equitable than myself. And further, I have never observed that any truth before unknown has been brought to light by the disputations that are practised in the schools; for while each strives for the victory, each is much more occupied in making the best of mere verisimilitude, than in weighing the reasons on both sides of the question; and those who have been long good advocates are not afterwards on that account the better judges.

As for the advantage that others would derive from the communication of my thoughts, it could not be very great; because I have not yet so far prosecuted them as that much does not remain to be added before they can be applied to practice. And I think I may say without vanity, that if there is any one who can carry them out that length, it must be myself rather than another: not that there may not be in the world many minds incomparably superior to mine, but because one cannot so well seize a thing and make it one's own, when it has been learned from another, as when one has himself discovered it. And so true is this of the present subject that, though I have often explained some of my opinions to persons of much acuteness, who, whilst I was speaking, appeared to understand them very distinctly, yet, when they repeated them, I have observed that they almost always changed them to such an extent that I could no longer acknowledge them as mine. I am glad, by the way, to take this opportunity of requesting posterity never to believe on hearsay that anything has proceeded from me which has not been published by myself; and I am not at all astonished at the extravagances attributed to those ancient philosophers whose own writings we do not possess; whose thoughts, however, I do not on that account suppose to have been really absurd, seeing they were among the ablest men of their times, but only that these have been falsely represented to us. It is observable, accordingly, that scarcely in a single instance has any one of their disciples surpassed them; and I am quite sure that the most devoted of the present followers of Aristotle would think themselves happy if they had as much knowledge of nature as he possessed, were it even under the condition that they should never afterwards attain to higher. In this respect they are like the ivy which never strives to rise above the tree that sustains it, and which frequently even returns downwards when it has reached the top; for it seems to me that they also sink, in other words, render themselves less wise than they would be if they gave up study, who, not contented with knowing all that is intelligibly explained in their author, desire in addition to find in him the solution of many difficulties of which he says not a word, and never perhaps so much as thought. Their fashion of philosophizing, however, is well suited to persons whose abilities fall below mediocrity; for the obscurity of the distinctions and principles of which they make use enables them to speak of all things with as much confidence as if they really knew them, and to defend all that they say on any subject against the most subtle and skillful, without its being possible for any one to convict them of error. In this they seem to me to be like a blind man, who, in order to fight on equal terms with a person that sees, should have made him descend to the bottom of an intensely dark cave: and I may say that such persons have an interest in my refraining from publishing the principles of the philosophy of which I make use; for, since these are of a kind the simplest and most evident, I should, by publishing them, do much the same as if I were to throw open the windows, and allow the light of day to enter the cave into which the combatants had descended. But even superior men have no reason for any great anxiety to know these principles, for if what they desire is to be able to speak of all things, and to acquire a reputation for learning, they will gain their end more easily by remaining satisfied with the appearance of truth, which can be found without much difficulty in all sorts of matters, than by seeking the truth itself which unfolds itself but slowly and that only in some departments, while it obliges us, when we have to speak of others, freely to confess our ignorance. If, however, they prefer the knowledge of some few truths to the vanity of appearing ignorant of none, as such knowledge is undoubtedly much to be preferred, and, if they choose to follow a course similar to mine, they do not require for this that I should say anything more than I have already said in this discourse. For if they are capable of making greater advancement than I have made, they will much more be able of themselves to discover all that I believe myself to have found; since as I have never examined aught except in order, it is certain that what yet remains to be discovered is in itself more difficult and recondite, than that which I have already been enabled to find, and the gratification would be much less in learning it from me than in discovering it for themselves. Besides this, the habit which they will acquire, by seeking first what is easy, and then passing onward slowly and step by step to the more difficult, will benefit them more than all my instructions. Thus, in my own case, I am persuaded that if I had been taught from my youth all the truths of which I have since sought out demonstrations, and had thus learned them without labour, I should never, perhaps, have known any beyond these; at least, I should never have acquired the habit and the facility which I think I possess in always discovering new truths in proportion as I give myself to the search. And, in a single word, if there is any work in the world which cannot be so well finished by another as by him who has commenced it, it is that at which I labour.

It is true, indeed, as regards the experiments which may conduce to this end, that one man is not equal to the task of making them all; but yet he can advantageously avail himself, in this work, of no hands besides his own, unless those of artisans, or parties of the same kind, whom he could pay, and whom the hope of gain (a means of great efficacy) might stimulate to accuracy in the performance of what was prescribed to them. For as to those who, through curiosity or a desire of learning, of their own accord, perhaps, offer him their services, besides that in general their promises exceed their performance, and that they sketch out fine designs of which not one is ever realized, they will, without doubt, expect to be compensated for their trouble by the explication of some difficulties, or, at least, by compliments and useless speeches, in which he cannot spend any portion of his time without loss to himself. And as for the experiments that others have already made, even although these parties should be willing of themselves to communicate them to him (which is what those who esteem them secrets will never do), the experiments are, for the most part, accompanied with so many circumstances and superfluous elements, as to make it exceedingly difficult to disentangle the truth from its adjuncts--besides, he will find almost all of them so ill described, or even so false (because those who made them have wished to see in them only such facts as they deemed conformable to their principles), that, if in the entire number there should be some of a nature suited to his purpose, still their value could not compensate for the time what would be necessary to make the selection. So that if there existed any one whom we assuredly knew to be capable of making discoveries of the highest kind, and of the greatest possible utility to the public; and if all other men were therefore eager by all means to assist him in successfully prosecuting his designs, I do not see that they could do aught else for him beyond contributing to defray the expenses of the experiments that might be necessary; and for the rest, prevent his being deprived of his leisure by the unseasonable interruptions of any one. But besides that I neither have so high an opinion of myself as to be willing to make promise of anything extraordinary, nor feed on imaginations so vain as to fancy that the public must be much interested in my designs; I do not, on the other hand, own a soul so mean as to be capable of accepting from any one a favor of which it could be supposed that I was unworthy.

These considerations taken together were the reason why, for the last three years, I have been unwilling to publish the treatise I had on hand, and why I even resolved to give publicity during my life to no other that was so general, or by which the principles of my physics might be understood. But since then, two other reasons have come into operation that have determined me here to subjoin some particular specimens, and give the public some account of my doings and designs. Of these considerations, the first is, that if I failed to do so, many who were cognizant of my previous intention to publish some writings, might have imagined that the reasons which induced me to refrain from so doing, were less to my credit than they really are; for although I am not immoderately desirous of glory, or even, if I may venture so to say, although I am averse from it in so far as I deem it hostile to repose which I hold in greater account than aught else, yet, at the same time, I have never sought to conceal my actions as if they were crimes, nor made use of many precautions that I might remain unknown; and this partly because I should have thought such a course of conduct a wrong against myself, and partly because it would have occasioned me some sort of uneasiness which would again have been contrary to the perfect mental tranquillity which I court. And forasmuch as, while thus indifferent to the thought alike of fame or of forgetfulness, I have yet been unable to prevent myself from acquiring some sort of reputation, I have thought it incumbent on me to do my best to save myself at least from being ill-spoken of. The other reason that has determined me to commit to writing these specimens of philosophy is, that I am becoming daily more and more alive to the delay which my design of self-instruction suffers, for want of the infinity of experiments I require, and which it is impossible for me to make without the assistance of others: and, without flattering myself so much as to expect the public to take a large share in my interests, I am yet unwilling to be found so far wanting in the duty I owe to myself, as to give occasion to those who shall survive me to make it matter of reproach against me some day, that I might have left them many things in a much more perfect state than I have done, had I not too much neglected to make them aware of the ways in which they could have promoted the accomplishment of my designs.

And I thought that it was easy for me to select some matters which should neither be obnoxious to much controversy, nor should compel me to expound more of my principles than I desired, and which should yet be sufficient clearly to exhibit what I can or cannot accomplish in the sciences. Whether or not I have succeeded in this it is not for me to say; and I do not wish to forestall the judgments of others by speaking myself of my writings; but it will gratify me if they be examined, and, to afford the greater inducement to this I request all who may have any objections to make to them, to take the trouble of forwarding these to my publisher, who will give me notice of them, that I may endeavor to subjoin at the same time my reply; and in this way readers seeing both at once will more easily determine where the truth lies; for I do not engage in any case to make prolix replies, but only with perfect frankness to avow my errors if I am convinced of them, or if I cannot perceive them, simply to state what I think is required for defense of the matters I have written, adding thereto no explication of any new matte that it may not be necessary to pass without end from one thing to another.

If some of the matters of which I have spoken in the beginning of the "Dioptrics" and "Meteorics" should offend at first sight, because I call them hypotheses and seem indifferent about giving proof of them, I request a patient and attentive reading of the whole, from which I hope those hesitating will derive satisfaction; for it appears to me that the reasonings are so mutually connected in these treatises, that, as the last are demonstrated by the first which are their causes, the first are in their turn demonstrated by the last which are their effects. Nor must it be imagined that I here commit the fallacy which the logicians call a circle; for since experience renders the majority of these effects most certain, the causes from which I deduce them do not serve so much to establish their reality as to explain their existence; but on the contrary, the reality of the causes is established by the reality of the effects. Nor have I called them hypotheses with any other end in view except that it may be known that I think I am able to deduce them from those first truths which I have already expounded; and yet that I have expressly determined not to do so, to prevent a certain class of minds from thence taking occasion to build some extravagant philosophy upon what they may take to be my principles, and my being blamed for it. I refer to those who imagine that they can master in a day all that another has taken twenty years to think out, as soon as he has spoken two or three words to them on the subject; or who are the more liable to error and the less capable of perceiving truth in very proportion as they are more subtle and lively. As to the opinions which are truly and wholly mine, I offer no apology for them as new,--persuaded as I am that if their reasons be well considered they will be found to be so simple and so conformed, to common sense as to appear less extraordinary and less paradoxical than any others which can be held on the same subjects; nor do I even boast of being the earliest discoverer of any of them, but only of having adopted them, neither because they had nor because they had not been held by others, but solely because reason has convinced me of their truth.

Though artisans may not be able at once to execute the invention which is explained in the "Dioptrics," I do not think that any one on that account is entitled to condemn it; for since address and practice are required in order so to make and adjust the machines described by me as not to overlook the smallest particular, I should not be less astonished if they succeeded on the first attempt than if a person were in one day to become an accomplished performer on the guitar, by merely having excellent sheets of music set up before him. And if I write in French, which is the language of my country, in preference to Latin, which is that of my preceptors, it is because I expect that those who make use of their unprejudiced natural reason will be better judges of my opinions than those who give heed to the writings of the ancients only; and as for those who unite good sense with habits of study, whom alone I desire for judges, they will not, I feel assured, be so partial to Latin as to refuse to listen to my reasonings merely because I expound them in the vulgar tongue.

In conclusion, I am unwilling here to say anything very specific of the progress which I expect to make for the future in the sciences, or to bind myself to the public by any promise which I am not certain of being able to fulfill; but this only will I say, that I have resolved to devote what time I may still have to live to no other occupation than that of endeavoring to acquire some knowledge of Nature, which shall be of such a kind as to enable us therefrom to deduce rules in medicine of greater certainty than those at present in use; and that my inclination is so much opposed to all other pursuits, especially to such as cannot be useful to some without being hurtful to others, that if, by any circumstances, I had been constrained to engage in such, I do not believe that I should have been able to succeed. Of this I here make a public declaration, though well aware that it cannot serve to procure for me any consideration in the world, which, however, I do not in the least affect; and I shall always hold myself more obliged to those through whose favor I am permitted to enjoy my retirement without interruption than to any who might offer me the highest earthly preferments.

MEDITATIONS ON FIRST PHILOSOPHY

by

Rene Descartes

Translated by John Veitch

INTRODUCTION
TO THE VERY SAGE AND ILLUSTRIOUS THE DEAN AND DOCTORS OF THE SACRED FACULTY OF THEOLOGY OF PARIS

GENTLEMEN,

1. The motive which impels me to present this Treatise to you is so reasonable, and when you shall learn its design, I am confident that you also will consider that there is ground so valid for your taking it under your protection, that I can in no way better recommend it to you than by briefly stating the end which I proposed to myself in it.

2. I have always been of the opinion that the two questions respecting God and the Soul were the chief of those that ought to be determined by help of Philosophy rather than of Theology; for although to us, the faithful, it be sufficient to hold as matters of faith, that the human soul does not perish with the body, and that God exists, it yet assuredly seems impossible ever to persuade infidels of the reality of any religion, or almost even any moral virtue, unless, first of all, those two things be proved to them by natural reason. And since in this life there are frequently greater rewards held out to vice than to virtue, few would prefer the right to the useful, if they were restrained neither by the fear of God nor the expectation of another life; and although it is quite true that the existence of God is to be believed since it is taught in the sacred Scriptures, and that, on the other hand, the sacred Scriptures are to be believed because they come from God (for since faith is a gift of God, the same Being who bestows grace to enable us to believe other things, can likewise impart of it to enable us to believe his own existence), nevertheless, this cannot be submitted to infidels, who would consider that the reasoning

proceeded in a circle. And, indeed, I have observed that you, with all the other theologians, not only affirmed the sufficiency of natural reason for the proof of the existence of God, but also, that it may be inferred from sacred Scripture, that the knowledge of God is much clearer than of many created things, and that it is really so easy of acquisition as to leave those who do not possess it blameworthy. This is manifest from these words of the Book of Wisdom, chap. xiii., where it is said, Howbeit they are not to be excused; for if their understanding was so great that they could discern the world and the creatures, why did they not rather find out the Lord thereof? And in Romans, chap. i., it is said that they are without excuse; and again, in the same place, by these words, That which may be known of God is manifest in them--we seem to be admonished that all which can be known of God may be made manifest by reasons obtained from no other source than the inspection of our own minds. I have, therefore, thought that it would not be unbecoming in me to inquire how and by what way, without going out of ourselves, God may be more easily and certainly known than the things of the world.

3. And as regards the Soul, although many have judged that its nature could not be easily discovered, and some have even ventured to say that human reason led to the conclusion that it perished with the body, and that the contrary opinion could be held through faith alone; nevertheless, since the Lateran Council, held under Leo X. (in session viii.), condemns these, and expressly enjoins Christian philosophers to refute their arguments, and establish the truth according to their ability, I have ventured to attempt it in this work.

4. Moreover, I am aware that most of the irreligious deny the existence of God, and the distinctness of the human soul from the body, for no other reason than because these points, as they allege, have never as yet been demonstrated. Now, although I am

by no means of their opinion, but, on the contrary, hold that almost all the proofs which have been adduced on these questions by great men, possess, when rightly understood, the force of demonstrations, and that it is next to impossible to discover new, yet there is, I apprehend, no more useful service to be performed in Philosophy, than if some one were, once for all, carefully to seek out the best of these reasons, and expound them so accurately and clearly that, for the future, it might be manifest to all that they are real demonstrations. And finally, since many persons were greatly desirous of this, who knew that I had cultivated a certain Method of resolving all kinds of difficulties in the sciences, which is not indeed new (there being nothing older than truth), but of which they were aware I had made successful use in other instances, I judged it to be my duty to make trial of it also on the present matter.

5. Now the sum of what I have been able to accomplish on the subject is contained in this Treatise. Not that I here essayed to collect all the diverse reasons which might be adduced as proofs on this subject, for this does not seem to be necessary, unless on matters where no one proof of adequate certainty is to be had; but I treated the first and chief alone in such a manner that I should venture now to propose them as demonstrations of the highest certainty and evidence. And I will also add that they are such as to lead me to think that there is no way open to the mind of man by which proofs superior to them can ever be discovered for the importance of the subject, and the glory of God, to which all this relates, constrain me to speak here somewhat more freely of myself than I have been accustomed to do. Nevertheless, whatever certitude and evidence I may find in these demonstrations, I cannot therefore persuade myself that they are level to the comprehension of all. But just as in geometry there are many of the demonstrations of Archimedes, Apollonius,

Pappus, and others, which, though received by all as evident even and certain (because indeed they manifestly contain nothing which, considered by itself, it is not very easy to understand, and no consequents that are inaccurately related to their antecedents), are nevertheless understood by a very limited number, because they are somewhat long, and demand the whole attention of the reader: so in the same way, although I consider the demonstrations of which I here make use, to be equal or even superior to the geometrical in certitude and evidence, I am afraid, nevertheless, that they will not be adequately understood by many, as well because they also are somewhat long and involved, as chiefly because they require the mind to be entirely free from prejudice, and able with ease to detach itself from the commerce of the senses. And, to speak the truth, the ability for metaphysical studies is less general than for those of geometry. And, besides, there is still this difference that, as in geometry, all are persuaded that nothing is usually advanced of which there is not a certain demonstration, those but partially versed in it err more frequently in assenting to what is false, from a desire of seeming to understand it, than in denying what is true. In philosophy, on the other hand, where it is believed that all is doubtful, few sincerely give themselves to the search after truth, and by far the greater number seek the reputation of bold thinkers by audaciously impugning such truths as are of the greatest moment.

6. Hence it is that, whatever force my reasonings may possess, yet because they belong to philosophy, I do not expect they will have much effect on the minds of men, unless you extend to them your patronage and approval. But since your Faculty is held in so great esteem by all, and since the name of SORBONNE is of such authority, that not only in matters of faith, but even also in what regards human philosophy, has the judgment of no other society, after the Sacred Councils, received

so great deference, it being the universal conviction that it is impossible elsewhere to find greater perspicacity and solidity, or greater wisdom and integrity in giving judgment, I doubt not, if you but condescend to pay so much regard to this Treatise as to be willing, in the first place, to correct it (for mindful not only of my humanity, but chiefly also of my ignorance, I do not affirm that it is free from errors); in the second place, to supply what is wanting in it, to perfect what is incomplete, and to give more ample illustration where it is demanded, or at least to indicate these defects to myself that I may endeavour to remedy them; and, finally, when the reasonings contained in it, by which the existence of God and the distinction of the human soul from the body are established, shall have been brought to such degree of perspicuity as to be esteemed exact demonstrations, of which I am assured they admit, if you condescend to accord them the authority of your approbation, and render a public testimony of their truth and certainty, I doubt not, I say, but that henceforward all the errors which have ever been entertained on these questions will very soon be effaced from the minds of men. For truth itself will readily lead the remainder of the ingenious and the learned to subscribe to your judgment; and your authority will cause the atheists, who are in general sciolists rather than ingenious or learned, to lay aside the spirit of contradiction, and lead them, perhaps, to do battle in their own persons for reasonings which they find considered demonstrations by all men of genius, lest they should seem not to understand them; and, finally, the rest of mankind will readily trust to so many testimonies, and there will no longer be any one who will venture to doubt either the existence of God or the real distinction of mind and body. It is for you, in your singular wisdom, to judge of the importance of the establishment of such beliefs, who are cognisant of the disorders which doubt of these truths produces. But it would not here become me to commend at greater length the cause of God and of religion to you, who have always proved the strongest support of the Catholic Church.

PREFACE TO THE READER

1. I have already slightly touched upon the questions respecting the existence of God and the nature of the human soul, in the "Discourse on the Method of rightly conducting the Reason, and seeking Truth in the Sciences," published in French in the year 1637; not however, with the design of there treating of them fully, but only, as it were, in passing, that I might learn from the judgment of my readers in what way I should afterward handle them; for these questions appeared to me to be of such moment as to be worthy of being considered more than once, and the path which I follow in discussing them is so little trodden, and so remote from the ordinary route that I thought it would not be expedient to illustrate it at greater length in French, and in a discourse that might be read by all, lest even the more feeble minds should believe that this path might be entered upon by them.

2. But, as in the " Discourse on Method," I had requested all who might find aught meriting censure in my writings, to do me the favor of pointing it out to me, I may state that no objections worthy of remark have been alleged against what I then said on these questions except two, to which I will here briefly reply, before undertaking their more detailed discussion.

3. The first objection is that though, while the human mind reflects on itself, it does not perceive that it is any other than a thinking thing, it does not follow that its nature or essence consists only in its being a thing which thinks; so that the word ONLY shall exclude all other things which might also perhaps be said to pertain to the nature of the mind. To this objection I reply, that it was not my intention in that place to exclude these according to the order of truth in the matter (of which I did not then treat), but only according to the order of thought

(perception); so that my meaning was, that I clearly apprehended nothing, so far as I was conscious, as belonging to my essence, except that I was a thinking thing, or a thing possessing in itself the faculty of thinking. But I will show hereafter how, from the consciousness that nothing besides thinking belongs to the essence of the mind, it follows that nothing else does in truth belong to it.

4. The second objection is that it does not follow, from my possessing the idea of a thing more perfect than I am, that the idea itself is more perfect than myself, and much less that what is represented by the idea exists. But I reply that in the term idea there is here something equivocal; for it may be taken either materially for an act of the understanding, and in this sense it cannot be said to be more perfect than I, or objectively, for the thing represented by that act, which, although it be not supposed to exist out of my understanding, may, nevertheless, be more perfect than myself, by reason of its essence. But, in the sequel of this treatise I will show more amply how, from my possessing the idea of a thing more perfect than myself, it follows that this thing really exists.

5. Besides these two objections, I have seen, indeed, two treatises of sufficient length relating to the present matter. In these, however, my conclusions, much more than my premises, were impugned, and that by arguments borrowed from the common places of the atheists. But, as arguments of this sort can make no impression on the minds of those who shall rightly understand my reasonings, and as the judgments of many are so irrational and weak that they are persuaded rather by the opinions on a subject that are first presented to them, however false and opposed to reason they may be, than by a true and solid, but subsequently received, refutation of them, I am unwilling here to reply to these strictures from a dread of being, in the first

instance, obliged to state them. I will only say, in general, that all which the atheists commonly allege in favor of the non-existence of God, arises continually from one or other of these two things, namely, either the ascription of human affections to Deity, or the undue attribution to our minds of so much vigor and wisdom that we may essay to determine and comprehend both what God can and ought to do; hence all that is alleged by them will occasion us no difficulty, provided only we keep in remembrance that our minds must be considered finite, while Deity is incomprehensible and infinite.

6. Now that I have once, in some measure, made proof of the opinions of men regarding my work, I again undertake to treat of God and the human soul, and at the same time to discuss the principles of the entire First Philosophy, without, however, expecting any commendation from the crowd for my endeavors, or a wide circle of readers. On the contrary, I would advise none to read this work, unless such as are able and willing to meditate with me in earnest, to detach their minds from commerce with the senses, and likewise to deliver themselves from all prejudice; and individuals of this character are, I well know, remarkably rare. But with regard to those who, without caring to comprehend the order and connection of the reasonings, shall study only detached clauses for the purpose of small but noisy criticism, as is the custom with many, I may say that such persons will not profit greatly by the reading of this treatise; and although perhaps they may find opportunity for cavilling in several places, they will yet hardly start any pressing objections, or such as shall be deserving of reply.

7. But since, indeed, I do not promise to satisfy others on all these subjects at first sight, nor arrogate so much to myself as to believe that I have been able to forsee all that may be the source of difficulty to each ones I shall expound, first of all, in the

Meditations, those considerations by which I feel persuaded that I have arrived at a certain and evident knowledge of truth, in order that I may ascertain whether the reasonings which have prevailed with myself will also be effectual in convincing others. I will then reply to the objections of some men, illustrious for their genius and learning, to whom these Meditations were sent for criticism before they were committed to the press; for these objections are so numerous and varied that I venture to anticipate that nothing, at least nothing of any moment, will readily occur to any mind which has not been touched upon in them. Hence it is that I earnestly entreat my readers not to come to any judgment on the questions raised in the Meditations until they have taken care to read the whole of the Objections, with the relative Replies.

SYNOPSIS OF THE SIX FOLLOWING MEDITATIONS

1. IN THE First Meditation I expound the grounds on which we may doubt in general of all things, and especially of material objects, so long at least, as we have no other foundations for the sciences than those we have hitherto possessed. Now, although the utility of a doubt so general may not be manifest at first sight, it is nevertheless of the greatest, since it delivers us from all prejudice, and affords the easiest pathway by which the mind may withdraw itself from the senses; and finally makes it impossible for us to doubt wherever we afterward discover truth.

2. In the Second, the mind which, in the exercise of the freedom peculiar to itself, supposes that no object is, of the existence of which it has even the slightest doubt, finds that, meanwhile, it must itself exist. And this point is likewise of the highest moment, for the mind is thus enabled easily to distinguish what pertains to itself, that is, to the intellectual nature, from what is to be referred to the body. But since some, perhaps, will

expect, at this stage of our progress, a statement of the reasons which establish the doctrine of the immortality of the soul, I think it proper here to make such aware, that it was my aim to write nothing of which I could not give exact demonstration, and that I therefore felt myself obliged to adopt an order similar to that in use among the geometers, viz., to premise all upon which the proposition in question depends, before coming to any conclusion respecting it. Now, the first and chief prerequisite for the knowledge of the immortality of the soul is our being able to form the clearest possible conception (conceptus--concept) of the soul itself, and such as shall be absolutely distinct from all our notions of body; and how this is to be accomplished is there shown. There is required, besides this, the assurance that all objects which we clearly and distinctly think are true (really exist) in that very mode in which we think them; and this could not be established previously to the Fourth Meditation. Farther, it is necessary, for the same purpose, that we possess a distinct conception of corporeal nature, which is given partly in the Second and partly in the Fifth and Sixth Meditations. And, finally, on these grounds, we are necessitated to conclude, that all those objects which are clearly and distinctly conceived to be diverse substances, as mind and body, are substances really reciprocally distinct; and this inference is made in the Sixth Meditation. The absolute distinction of mind and body is, besides, confirmed in this Second Meditation, by showing that we cannot conceive body unless as divisible; while, on the other hand, mind cannot be conceived unless as indivisible. For we are not able to conceive the half of a mind, as we can of any body, however small, so that the natures of these two substances are to be held, not only as diverse, but even in some measure as contraries. I have not, however, pursued this discussion further in the present treatise, as well for the reason that these considerations are sufficient to show that the destruction of the mind does not follow from the corruption of the body, and thus to afford to men the hope of a future life, as also because the premises from which it is competent for us to infer the immortality of the soul, involve an explication of the whole principles of Physics: in order to establish, in the first place, that generally all substances, that is, all things which can exist only in consequence of having been created by God, are in their own nature incorruptible, and can never cease to be, unless God himself, by refusing his concurrence to them, reduce them to nothing; and, in the second place, that body, taken generally, is a substance, and therefore can never perish, but that the human body, in as far as it differs from other bodies, is constituted only by a certain configuration of members, and by other accidents of this sort, while the human mind is not made up of accidents, but is a pure substance. For although all the accidents of the mind be changed-- although, for example, it think certain things, will others, and perceive others, the mind itself does not vary with these changes; while, on the contrary, the human body is no longer the same if a change take place in the form of any of its parts: from which it follows that the body may, indeed, without difficulty perish, but that the mind is in its own nature immortal.

3. In the Third Meditation, I have unfolded at sufficient length, as appears to me, my chief argument for the existence of God. But yet, since I was there desirous to avoid the use of comparisons taken from material objects, that I might withdraw, as far as possible, the minds of my readers from the senses, numerous obscurities perhaps remain, which, however, will, I trust, be afterward entirely removed in the Replies to the Objections: thus among other things, it may be difficult to understand how the idea of a being absolutely perfect, which is found in our minds, possesses so much objective reality i.e.,

participates by representation in so many degrees of being and perfection that it must be held to arise from a cause absolutely perfect. This is illustrated in the Replies by the comparison of a highly perfect machine, the idea of which exists in the mind of some workman; for as the objective (i.e., representative) perfection of this idea must have some cause, viz, either the science of the workman, or of some other person from whom he has received the idea, in the same way the idea of God, which is found in us, demands God himself for its cause.

4. In the Fourth, it is shown that all which we clearly and distinctly perceive (apprehend) is true; and, at the same time, is explained wherein consists the nature of error, points that require to be known as well for confirming the preceding truths, as for the better understanding of those that are to follow. But, meanwhile, it must be observed, that I do not at all there treat of Sin, that is, of error committed in the pursuit of good and evil, but of that sort alone which arises in the determination of the true and the false. Nor do I refer to matters of faith, or to the conduct of life, but only to what regards speculative truths, and such as are known by means of the natural light alone.

5. In the Fifth, besides the illustration of corporeal nature, taken generically, a new demonstration is given of the existence of God, not free, perhaps, any more than the former, from certain difficulties, but of these the solution will be found in the Replies to the Objections. I further show, in what sense it is true that the certitude of geometrical demonstrations themselves is dependent on the knowledge of God.

6. Finally, in the Sixth, the act of the understanding (intellectio) is distinguished from that of the imagination (imaginatio); the marks of this distinction are described; the human mind is shown to be really distinct from the body, and, nevertheless, to be so closely conjoined therewith, as together to

form, as it were, a unity. The whole of the errors which arise from the senses are brought under review, while the means of avoiding them are pointed out; and, finally, all the grounds are adduced from which the existence of material objects may be inferred; not, however, because I deemed them of great utility in establishing what they prove, viz., that there is in reality a world, that men are possessed of bodies, and the like, the truth of which no one of sound mind ever seriously doubted; but because, from a close consideration of them, it is perceived that they are neither so strong nor clear as the reasonings which conduct us to the knowledge of our mind and of God; so that the latter are, of all which come under human knowledge, the most certain and manifest-- a conclusion which it was my single aim in these Meditations to establish; on which account I here omit mention of the various other questions which, in the course of the discussion, I had occasion likewise to consider.

MEDITATION I
OF THE THINGS OF WHICH WE MAY DOUBT

1. SEVERAL years have now elapsed since I first became aware that I had accepted, even from my youth, many false opinions for true, and that consequently what I afterward based on such principles was highly doubtful; and from that time I was convinced of the necessity of undertaking once in my life to rid myself of all the opinions I had adopted, and of commencing anew the work of building from the foundation, if I desired to establish a firm and abiding superstructure in the sciences. But as this enterprise appeared to me to be one of great magnitude, I waited until I had attained an age so mature as to leave me no hope that at any stage of life more advanced I should be better able to execute my design. On this account, I have delayed so long that I should henceforth consider I was doing wrong were I still to consume in deliberation any of the time that now remains for action. To-day, then, since I have opportunely freed my mind from all cares and am happily disturbed by no passions, and since I am in the secure possession of leisure in a peaceable retirement, I will at length apply myself earnestly and freely to the general overthrow of all my former opinions.

2. But, to this end, it will not be necessary for me to show that the whole of these are false--a point, perhaps, which I shall never reach; but as even now my reason convinces me that I ought not the less carefully to withhold belief from what is not entirely certain and indubitable, than from what is manifestly false, it will be sufficient to justify the rejection of the whole if I shall find in each some ground for doubt. Nor for this purpose will it be necessary even to deal with each belief individually, which would be truly an endless labor; but, as the removal from below of the foundation necessarily involves the downfall of the whole edifice,

I will at once approach the criticism of the principles on which all my former beliefs rested.

3. All that I have, up to this moment, accepted as possessed of the highest truth and certainty, I received either from or through the senses. I observed, however, that these sometimes misled us; and it is the part of prudence not to place absolute confidence in that by which we have even once been deceived.

4. But it may be said, perhaps, that, although the senses occasionally mislead us respecting minute objects, and such as are so far removed from us as to be beyond the reach of close observation, there are yet many other of their informations (presentations), of the truth of which it is manifestly impossible to doubt; as for example, that I am in this place, seated by the fire, clothed in a winter dressing gown, that I hold in my hands this piece of paper, with other intimations of the same nature. But how could I deny that I possess these hands and this body, and withal escape being classed with persons in a state of insanity, whose brains are so disordered and clouded by dark bilious vapors as to cause them pertinaciously to assert that they are monarchs when they are in the greatest poverty; or clothed in gold and purple when destitute of any covering; or that their head is made of clay, their body of glass, or that they are gourds? I should certainly be not less insane than they, were I to regulate my procedure according to examples so extravagant.

5. Though this be true, I must nevertheless here consider that I am a man, and that, consequently, I am in the habit of sleeping, and representing to myself in dreams those same things, or even sometimes others less probable, which the insane think are presented to them in their waking moments. How often have I dreamt that I was in these familiar circumstances, that I was dressed, and occupied this place by the fire, when I was lying undressed in bed? At the present moment, however, I certainly

look upon this paper with eyes wide awake; the head which I now move is not asleep; I extend this hand consciously and with express purpose, and I perceive it; the occurrences in sleep are not so distinct as all this. But I cannot forget that, at other times I have been deceived in sleep by similar illusions; and, attentively considering those cases, I perceive so clearly that there exist no certain marks by which the state of waking can ever be distinguished from sleep, that I feel greatly astonished; and in amazement I almost persuade myself that I am now dreaming.

6. Let us suppose, then, that we are dreaming, and that all these particulars--namely, the opening of the eyes, the motion of the head, the forth- putting of the hands--are merely illusions; and even that we really possess neither an entire body nor hands such as we see. Nevertheless it must be admitted at least that the objects which appear to us in sleep are, as it were, painted representations which could not have been formed unless in the likeness of realities; and, therefore, that those general objects, at all events, namely, eyes, a head, hands, and an entire body, are not simply imaginary, but really existent. For, in truth, painters themselves, even when they study to represent sirens and satyrs by forms the most fantastic and extraordinary, cannot bestow upon them natures absolutely new, but can only make a certain medley of the members of different animals; or if they chance to imagine something so novel that nothing at all similar has ever been seen before, and such as is, therefore, purely fictitious and absolutely false, it is at least certain that the colors of which this is composed are real. And on the same principle, although these general objects, viz. a body, eyes, a head, hands, and the like, be imaginary, we are nevertheless absolutely necessitated to admit the reality at least of some other objects still more simple and universal than these, of which, just as of certain real colors, all those images of things, whether true and real, or false and

fantastic, that are found in our consciousness (cogitatio), are formed.

7. To this class of objects seem to belong corporeal nature in general and its extension; the figure of extended things, their quantity or magnitude, and their number, as also the place in, and the time during, which they exist, and other things of the same sort.

8. We will not, therefore, perhaps reason illegitimately if we conclude from this that Physics, Astronomy, Medicine, and all the other sciences that have for their end the consideration of composite objects, are indeed of a doubtful character; but that Arithmetic, Geometry, and the other sciences of the same class, which regard merely the simplest and most general objects, and scarcely inquire whether or not these are really existent, contain somewhat that is certain and indubitable: for whether I am awake or dreaming, it remains true that two and three make five, and that a square has but four sides; nor does it seem possible that truths so apparent can ever fall under a suspicion of falsity or incertitude.

9. Nevertheless, the belief that there is a God who is all powerful, and who created me, such as I am, has, for a long time, obtained steady possession of my mind. How, then, do I know that he has not arranged that there should be neither earth, nor sky, nor any extended thing, nor figure, nor magnitude, nor place, providing at the same time, however, for the rise in me of the perceptions of all these objects, and the persuasion that these do not exist otherwise than as I perceive them ? And further, as I sometimes think that others are in error respecting matters of which they believe themselves to possess a perfect knowledge, how do I know that I am not also deceived each time I add together two and three, or number the sides of a square, or form some judgment still more simple, if more simple indeed can be

imagined? But perhaps Deity has not been willing that I should be thus deceived, for he is said to be supremely good. If, however, it were repugnant to the goodness of Deity to have created me subject to constant deception, it would seem likewise to be contrary to his goodness to allow me to be occasionally deceived; and yet it is clear that this is permitted.

10. Some, indeed, might perhaps be found who would be disposed rather to deny the existence of a Being so powerful than to believe that there is nothing certain. But let us for the present refrain from opposing this opinion, and grant that all which is here said of a Deity is fabulous: nevertheless, in whatever way it be supposed that I reach the state in which I exist, whether by fate, or chance, or by an endless series of antecedents and consequents, or by any other means, it is clear (since to be deceived and to err is a certain defect) that the probability of my being so imperfect as to be the constant victim of deception, will be increased exactly in proportion as the power possessed by the cause, to which they assign my origin, is lessened. To these reasonings I have assuredly nothing to reply, but am constrained at last to avow that there is nothing of all that I formerly believed to be true of which it is impossible to doubt, and that not through thoughtlessness or levity, but from cogent and maturely considered reasons; so that henceforward, if I desire to discover anything certain, I ought not the less carefully to refrain from assenting to those same opinions than to what might be shown to be manifestly false.

11. But it is not sufficient to have made these observations; care must be taken likewise to keep them in remembrance. For those old and customary opinions perpetually recur-- long and familiar usage giving them the right of occupying my mind, even almost against my will, and subduing my belief; nor will I lose the habit of deferring to them and confiding in them so long as I

shall consider them to be what in truth they are, viz, opinions to some extent doubtful, as I have already shown, but still highly probable, and such as it is much more reasonable to believe than deny. It is for this reason I am persuaded that I shall not be doing wrong, if, taking an opposite judgment of deliberate design, I become my own deceiver, by supposing, for a time, that all those opinions are entirely false and imaginary, until at length, having thus balanced my old by my new prejudices, my judgment shall no longer be turned aside by perverted usage from the path that may conduct to the perception of truth. For I am assured that, meanwhile, there will arise neither peril nor error from this course, and that I cannot for the present yield too much to distrust, since the end I now seek is not action but knowledge.

12. I will suppose, then, not that Deity, who is sovereignly good and the fountain of truth, but that some malignant demon, who is at once exceedingly potent and deceitful, has employed all his artifice to deceive me; I will suppose that the sky, the air, the earth, colors, figures, sounds, and all external things, are nothing better than the illusions of dreams, by means of which this being has laid snares for my credulity; I will consider myself as without hands, eyes, flesh, blood, or any of the senses, and as falsely believing that I am possessed of these; I will continue resolutely fixed in this belief, and if indeed by this means it be not in my power to arrive at the knowledge of truth, I shall at least do what is in my power, viz, suspend my judgment , and guard with settled purpose against giving my assent to what is false, and being imposed upon by this deceiver, whatever be his power and artifice. But this undertaking is arduous, and a certain indolence insensibly leads me back to my ordinary course of life; and just as the captive, who, perchance, was enjoying in his dreams an imaginary liberty, when he begins to suspect that it is but a vision, dreads awakening, and conspires with the agreeable illusions that

the deception may be prolonged; so I, of my own accord, fall back into the train of my former beliefs, and fear to arouse myself from my slumber, lest the time of laborious wakefulness that would succeed this quiet rest, in place of bringing any light of day, should prove inadequate to dispel the darkness that will arise from the difficulties that have now been raised.

MEDITATION II
OF THE NATURE OF THE HUMAN MIND; AND THAT IT IS MORE EASILY KNOWN THAN THE BODY

1. The Meditation of yesterday has filled my mind with so many doubts, that it is no longer in my power to forget them. Nor do I see, meanwhile, any principle on which they can be resolved; and, just as if I had fallen all of a sudden into very deep water, I am so greatly disconcerted as to be unable either to plant my feet firmly on the bottom or sustain myself by swimming on the surface. I will, nevertheless, make an effort, and try anew the same path on which I had entered yesterday, that is, proceed by casting aside all that admits of the slightest doubt, not less than if I had discovered it to be absolutely false; and I will continue always in this track until I shall find something that is certain, or at least, if I can do nothing more, until I shall know with certainty that there is nothing certain. Archimedes, that he might transport the entire globe from the place it occupied to another, demanded only a point that was firm and immovable; so, also, I shall be entitled to entertain the highest expectations, if I am fortunate enough to discover only one thing that is certain and indubitable.

2. I suppose, accordingly, that all the things which I see are false (fictitious); I believe that none of those objects which my fallacious memory represents ever existed; I suppose that I possess no senses; I believe that body, figure, extension, motion, and place are merely fictions of my mind. What is there, then, that can be esteemed true? Perhaps this only, that there is absolutely nothing certain.

3. But how do I know that there is not something different altogether from the objects I have now enumerated, of which it is impossible to entertain the slightest doubt? Is there not a God, or some being, by whatever name I may designate him, who causes

these thoughts to arise in my mind? But why suppose such a being, for it may be I myself am capable of producing them? Am I, then, at least not something? But I before denied that I possessed senses or a body; I hesitate, however, for what follows from that? Am I so dependent on the body and the senses that without these I cannot exist? But I had the persuasion that there was absolutely nothing in the world, that there was no sky and no earth, neither minds nor bodies; was I not, therefore, at the same time, persuaded that I did not exist? Far from it; I assuredly existed, since I was persuaded. But there is I know not what being, who is possessed at once of the highest power and the deepest cunning, who is constantly employing all his ingenuity in deceiving me. Doubtless, then, I exist, since I am deceived; and, let him deceive me as he may, he can never bring it about that I am nothing, so long as I shall be conscious that I am something. So that it must, in fine, be maintained, all things being maturely and carefully considered, that this proposition (pronunciatum) I am, I exist, is necessarily true each time it is expressed by me, or conceived in my mind.

4. But I do not yet know with sufficient clearness what I am, though assured that I am; and hence, in the next place, I must take care, lest perchance I inconsiderately substitute some other object in room of what is properly myself, and thus wander from truth, even in that knowledge (cognition) which I hold to be of all others the most certain and evident. For this reason, I will now consider anew what I formerly believed myself to be, before I entered on the present train of thought; and of my previous opinion I will retrench all that can in the least be invalidated by the grounds of doubt I have adduced, in order that there may at length remain nothing but what is certain and indubitable.

5. What then did I formerly think I was? Undoubtedly I judged that I was a man. But what is a man? Shall I say a rational

animal? Assuredly not; for it would be necessary forthwith to inquire into what is meant by animal, and what by rational, and thus, from a single question, I should insensibly glide into others, and these more difficult than the first; nor do I now possess enough of leisure to warrant me in wasting my time amid subtleties of this sort. I prefer here to attend to the thoughts that sprung up of themselves in my mind, and were inspired by my own nature alone, when I applied myself to the consideration of what I was. In the first place, then, I thought that I possessed a countenance, hands, arms, and all the fabric of members that appears in a corpse, and which I called by the name of body. It further occurred to me that I was nourished, that I walked, perceived, and thought, and all those actions I referred to the soul; but what the soul itself was I either did not stay to consider, or, if I did, I imagined that it was something extremely rare and subtile, like wind, or flame, or ether, spread through my grosser parts. As regarded the body, I did not even doubt of its nature, but thought I distinctly knew it, and if I had wished to describe it according to the notions I then entertained, I should have explained myself in this manner: By body I understand all that can be terminated by a certain figure; that can be comprised in a certain place, and so fill a certain space as therefrom to exclude every other body; that can be perceived either by touch, sight, hearing, taste, or smell; that can be moved in different ways, not indeed of itself, but by something foreign to it by which it is touched and from which it receives the impression; for the power of self-motion, as likewise that of perceiving and thinking, I held as by no means pertaining to the nature of body; on the contrary, I was somewhat astonished to find such faculties existing in some bodies.

6. But as to myself, what can I now say that I am, since I suppose there exists an extremely powerful, and, if I may so speak,

malignant being, whose whole endeavors are directed toward deceiving me? Can I affirm that I possess any one of all those attributes of which I have lately spoken as belonging to the nature of body? After attentively considering them in my own mind, I find none of them that can properly be said to belong to myself. To recount them were idle and tedious. Let us pass, then, to the attributes of the soul. The first mentioned were the powers of nutrition and walking; but, if it be true that I have no body, it is true likewise that I am capable neither of walking nor of being nourished. Perception is another attribute of the soul; but perception too is impossible without the body; besides, I have frequently, during sleep, believed that I perceived objects which I afterward observed I did not in reality perceive. Thinking is another attribute of the soul; and here I discover what properly belongs to myself. This alone is inseparable from me. I am--I exist: this is certain; but how often? As often as I think; for perhaps it would even happen, if I should wholly cease to think, that I should at the same time altogether cease to be. I now admit nothing that is not necessarily true. I am therefore, precisely speaking, only a thinking thing, that is, a mind (mens sive animus), understanding, or reason, terms whose signification was before unknown to me. I am, however, a real thing, and really existent; but what thing? The answer was, a thinking thing.

7. The question now arises, am I aught besides? I will stimulate my imagination with a view to discover whether I am not still something more than a thinking being. Now it is plain I am not the assemblage of members called the human body; I am not a thin and penetrating air diffused through all these members, or wind, or flame, or vapor, or breath, or any of all the things I can imagine; for I supposed that all these were not, and, without changing the supposition, I find that I still feel assured of my existence. But it is true, perhaps, that those very things which I

suppose to be non-existent, because they are unknown to me, are not in truth different from myself whom I know. This is a point I cannot determine, and do not now enter into any dispute regarding it. I can only judge of things that are known to me: I am conscious that I exist, and I who know that I exist inquire into what I am. It is, however, perfectly certain that the knowledge of my existence, thus precisely taken, is not dependent on things, the existence of which is as yet unknown to me: and consequently it is not dependent on any of the things I can feign in imagination. Moreover, the phrase itself, I frame an image (efffingo), reminds me of my error; for I should in truth frame one if I were to imagine myself to be anything, since to imagine is nothing more than to contemplate the figure or image of a corporeal thing; but I already know that I exist, and that it is possible at the same time that all those images, and in general all that relates to the nature of body, are merely dreams or chimeras. From this I discover that it is not more reasonable to say, I will excite my imagination that I may know more distinctly what I am, than to express myself as follows: I am now awake, and perceive something real; but because my perception is not sufficiently clear, I will of express purpose go to sleep that my dreams may represent to me the object of my perception with more truth and clearness. And, therefore, I know that nothing of all that I can embrace in imagination belongs to the knowledge which I have of myself, and that there is need to recall with the utmost care the mind from this mode of thinking, that it may be able to know its own nature with perfect distinctness.

8. But what, then, am I? A thinking thing, it has been said. But what is a thinking thing? It is a thing that doubts, understands, conceives, affirms, denies, wills, refuses; that imagines also, and perceives.

9. Assuredly it is not little, if all these properties belong to my nature. But why should they not belong to it? Am I not that very being who now doubts of almost everything; who, for all that, understands and conceives certain things; who affirms one alone as true, and denies the others; who desires to know more of them, and does not wish to be deceived; who imagines many things, sometimes even despite his will; and is likewise percipient of many, as if through the medium of the senses. Is there nothing of all this as true as that I am, even although I should be always dreaming, and although he who gave me being employed all his ingenuity to deceive me? Is there also any one of these attributes that can be properly distinguished from my thought, or that can be said to be separate from myself? For it is of itself so evident that it is I who doubt, I who understand, and I who desire, that it is here unnecessary to add anything by way of rendering it more clear. And I am as certainly the same being who imagines; for although it may be (as I before supposed) that nothing I imagine is true, still the power of imagination does not cease really to exist in me and to form part of my thought. In fine, I am the same being who perceives, that is, who apprehends certain objects as by the organs of sense, since, in truth, I see light, hear a noise, and feel heat. But it will be said that these presentations are false, and that I am dreaming. Let it be so. At all events it is certain that I seem to see light, hear a noise, and feel heat; this cannot be false, and this is what in me is properly called perceiving (sentire), which is nothing else than thinking.

10. From this I begin to know what I am with somewhat greater clearness and distinctness than heretofore. But, nevertheless, it still seems to me, and I cannot help believing, that corporeal things, whose images are formed by thought which fall under the senses, and are examined by the same, are known with much greater distinctness than that I know not what part of

myself which is not imaginable; although, in truth, it may seem strange to say that I know and comprehend with greater distinctness things whose existence appears to me doubtful, that are unknown, and do not belong to me, than others of whose reality I am persuaded, that are known to me, and appertain to my proper nature; in a word, than myself. But I see clearly what is the state of the case. My mind is apt to wander, and will not yet submit to be restrained within the limits of truth. Let us therefore leave the mind to itself once more, and, according to it every kind of liberty permit it to consider the objects that appear to it from without, in order that, having afterward withdrawn it from these gently and opportunely and fixed it on the consideration of its being and the properties it finds in itself, it may then be the more easily controlled.

11. Let us now accordingly consider the objects that are commonly thought to be the most easily, and likewise the most distinctly known, viz, the bodies we touch and see; not, indeed, bodies in general, for these general notions are usually somewhat more confused, but one body in particular. Take, for example, this piece of wax; it is quite fresh, having been but recently taken from the beehive; it has not yet lost the sweetness of the honey it contained; it still retains somewhat of the odor of the flowers from which it was gathered; its color, figure, size, are apparent (to the sight); it is hard, cold, easily handled; and sounds when struck upon with the finger. In fine, all that contributes to make a body as distinctly known as possible, is found in the one before us. But, while I am speaking, let it be placed near the fire--what remained of the taste exhales, the smell evaporates, the color changes, its figure is destroyed, its size increases, it becomes liquid, it grows hot, it can hardly be handled, and, although struck upon, it emits no sound. Does the same wax still remain after this change? It must be admitted that it does remain; no one doubts it, or judges

otherwise. What, then, was it I knew with so much distinctness in the piece of wax? Assuredly, it could be nothing of all that I observed by means of the senses, since all the things that fell under taste, smell, sight, touch, and hearing are changed, and yet the same wax remains.

12. It was perhaps what I now think, viz, that this wax was neither the sweetness of honey, the pleasant odor of flowers, the whiteness, the figure, nor the sound, but only a body that a little before appeared to me conspicuous under these forms, and which is now perceived under others. But, to speak precisely, what is it that I imagine when I think of it in this way? Let it be attentively considered, and, retrenching all that does not belong to the wax, let us see what remains. There certainly remains nothing, except something extended, flexible, and movable. But what is meant by flexible and movable? Is it not that I imagine that the piece of wax, being round, is capable of becoming square, or of passing from a square into a triangular figure? Assuredly such is not the case, because I conceive that it admits of an infinity of similar changes; and I am, moreover, unable to compass this infinity by imagination, and consequently this conception which I have of the wax is not the product of the faculty of imagination. But what now is this extension? Is it not also unknown? for it becomes greater when the wax is melted, greater when it is boiled, and greater still when the heat increases; and I should not conceive clearly and according to truth, the wax as it is, if I did not suppose that the piece we are considering admitted even of a wider variety of extension than I ever imagined, I must, therefore, admit that I cannot even comprehend by imagination what the piece of wax is, and that it is the mind alone (mens, Lat., entendement, F.) which perceives it. I speak of one piece in particular; for as to wax in general, this is still more evident. But what is the piece of wax that can be perceived only by the

understanding or mind? It is certainly the same which I see, touch, imagine; and, in fine, it is the same which, from the beginning, I believed it to be. But (and this it is of moment to observe) the perception of it is neither an act of sight, of touch, nor of imagination, and never was either of these, though it might formerly seem so, but is simply an intuition (inspectio) of the mind, which may be imperfect and confused, as it formerly was, or very clear and distinct, as it is at present, according as the attention is more or less directed to the elements which it contains, and of which it is composed.

13. But, meanwhile, I feel greatly astonished when I observe the weakness of my mind, and its proneness to error. For although, without at all giving expression to what I think, I consider all this in my own mind, words yet occasionally impede my progress, and I am almost led into error by the terms of ordinary language. We say, for example, that we see the same wax when it is before us, and not that we judge it to be the same from its retaining the same color and figure: whence I should forthwith be disposed to conclude that the wax is known by the act of sight, and not by the intuition of the mind alone, were it not for the analogous instance of human beings passing on in the street below, as observed from a window. In this case I do not fail to say that I see the men themselves, just as I say that I see the wax; and yet what do I see from the window beyond hats and cloaks that might cover artificial machines, whose motions might be determined by springs? But I judge that there are human beings from these appearances, and thus I comprehend, by the faculty of judgment alone which is in the mind, what I believed I saw with my eyes.

14. The man who makes it his aim to rise to knowledge superior to the common, ought to be ashamed to seek occasions of doubting from the vulgar forms of speech: instead, therefore,

of doing this, I shall proceed with the matter in hand, and inquire whether I had a clearer and more perfect perception of the piece of wax when I first saw it, and when I thought I knew it by means of the external sense itself, or, at all events, by the common sense (sensus communis), as it is called, that is, by the imaginative faculty; or whether I rather apprehend it more clearly at present, after having examined with greater care, both what it is, and in what way it can be known. It would certainly be ridiculous to entertain any doubt on this point. For what, in that first perception, was there distinct? What did I perceive which any animal might not have perceived? But when I distinguish the wax from its exterior forms, and when, as if I had stripped it of its vestments, I consider it quite naked, it is certain, although some error may still be found in my judgment, that I cannot, nevertheless, thus apprehend it without possessing a human mind.

15. But finally, what shall I say of the mind itself, that is, of myself? For as yet I do not admit that I am anything but mind. What, then! I who seem to possess so distinct an apprehension of the piece of wax, do I not know myself, both with greater truth and certitude, and also much more distinctly and clearly? For if I judge that the wax exists because I see it, it assuredly follows, much more evidently, that I myself am or exist, for the same reason: for it is possible that what I see may not in truth be wax, and that I do not even possess eyes with which to see anything; but it cannot be that when I see, or, which comes to the same thing, when I think I see, I myself who think am nothing. So likewise, if I judge that the wax exists because I touch it, it will still also follow that I am; and if I determine that my imagination, or any other cause, whatever it be, persuades me of the existence of the wax, I will still draw the same conclusion. And what is here remarked of the piece of wax, is applicable to all the other things that are external to me. And further, if the notion or perception

of wax appeared to me more precise and distinct, after that not only sight and touch, but many other causes besides, rendered it manifest to my apprehension, with how much greater distinctness must I now know myself, since all the reasons that contribute to the knowledge of the nature of wax, or of any body whatever, manifest still better the nature of my mind? And there are besides so many other things in the mind itself that contribute to the illustration of its nature, that those dependent on the body, to which I have here referred, scarcely merit to be taken into account.

16. But, in conclusion, I find I have insensibly reverted to the point I desired; for, since it is now manifest to me that bodies themselves are not properly perceived by the senses nor by the faculty of imagination, but by the intellect alone; and since they are not perceived because they are seen and touched, but only because they are understood or rightly comprehended by thought, I readily discover that there is nothing more easily or clearly apprehended than my own mind. But because it is difficult to rid one's self so promptly of an opinion to which one has been long accustomed, it will be desirable to tarry for some time at this stage, that, by long continued meditation, I may more deeply impress upon my memory this new knowledge.

MEDITATION III
OF GOD: THAT HE EXISTS

1. I WILL now close my eyes, I will stop my ears, I will turn away my senses from their objects, I will even efface from my consciousness all the images of corporeal things; or at least, because this can hardly be accomplished, I will consider them as empty and false; and thus, holding converse only with myself, and closely examining my nature, I will endeavor to obtain by degrees a more intimate and familiar knowledge of myself. I am a thinking (conscious) thing, that is, a being who doubts, affirms, denies, knows a few objects, and is ignorant of many,-- who loves, hates, wills, refuses, who imagines likewise, and perceives; for, as I before remarked, although the things which I perceive or imagine are perhaps nothing at all apart from me and in themselves, I am nevertheless assured that those modes of consciousness which I call perceptions and imaginations, in as far only as they are modes of consciousness, exist in me.

2. And in the little I have said I think I have summed up all that I really know, or at least all that up to this time I was aware I knew. Now, as I am endeavoring to extend my knowledge more widely, I will use circumspection, and consider with care whether I can still discover in myself anything further which I have not yet hitherto observed. I am certain that I am a thinking thing; but do I not therefore likewise know what is required to render me certain of a truth? In this first knowledge, doubtless, there is nothing that gives me assurance of its truth except the clear and distinct perception of what I affirm, which would not indeed be sufficient to give me the assurance that what I say is true, if it could ever happen that anything I thus clearly and distinctly perceived should prove false; and accordingly it seems to me that

I may now take as a general rule, that all that is very clearly and distinctly apprehended (conceived) is true.

3. Nevertheless I before received and admitted many things as wholly certain and manifest, which yet I afterward found to be doubtful. What, then, were those? They were the earth, the sky, the stars, and all the other objects which I was in the habit of perceiving by the senses. But what was it that I clearly and distinctly perceived in them? Nothing more than that the ideas and the thoughts of those objects were presented to my mind. And even now I do not deny that these ideas are found in my mind. But there was yet another thing which I affirmed, and which, from having been accustomed to believe it, I thought I clearly perceived, although, in truth, I did not perceive it at all; I mean the existence of objects external to me, from which those ideas proceeded, and to which they had a perfect resemblance; and it was here I was mistaken, or if I judged correctly, this assuredly was not to be traced to any knowledge I possessed (the force of my perception, Lat.).

4. But when I considered any matter in arithmetic and geometry, that was very simple and easy, as, for example, that two and three added together make five, and things of this sort, did I not view them with at least sufficient clearness to warrant me in affirming their truth? Indeed, if I afterward judged that we ought to doubt of these things, it was for no other reason than because it occurred to me that a God might perhaps have given me such a nature as that I should be deceived, even respecting the matters that appeared to me the most evidently true. But as often as this preconceived opinion of the sovereign power of a God presents itself to my mind, I am constrained to admit that it is easy for him, if he wishes it, to cause me to err, even in matters where I think I possess the highest evidence; and, on the other hand, as often as I direct my attention to things which I think I apprehend

with great clearness, I am so persuaded of their truth that I naturally break out into expressions such as these: Deceive me who may, no one will yet ever be able to bring it about that I am not, so long as I shall be conscious that I am, or at any future time cause it to be true that I have never been, it being now true that I am, or make two and three more or less than five, in supposing which, and other like absurdities, I discover a manifest contradiction. And in truth, as I have no ground for believing that Deity is deceitful, and as, indeed, I have not even considered the reasons by which the existence of a Deity of any kind is established, the ground of doubt that rests only on this supposition is very slight, and, so to speak, metaphysical. But, that I may be able wholly to remove it, I must inquire whether there is a God, as soon as an opportunity of doing so shall present itself; and if I find that there is a God, I must examine likewise whether he can be a deceiver; for, without the knowledge of these two truths, I do not see that I can ever be certain of anything. And that I may be enabled to examine this without interrupting the order of meditation I have proposed to myself which is, to pass by degrees from the notions that I shall find first in my mind to those I shall afterward discover in it, it is necessary at this stage to divide all my thoughts into certain classes, and to consider in which of these classes truth and error are, strictly speaking, to be found.

5. Of my thoughts some are, as it were, images of things, and to these alone properly belongs the name IDEA; as when I think represent to my mind a man, a chimera, the sky, an angel or God. Others, again, have certain other forms; as when I will, fear, affirm, or deny, I always, indeed, apprehend something as the object of my thought, but I also embrace in thought something more than the representation of the object; and of this class of

thoughts some are called volitions or affections, and others judgments.

6. Now, with respect to ideas, if these are considered only in themselves, and are not referred to any object beyond them, they cannot, properly speaking, be false; for, whether I imagine a goat or chimera, it is not less true that I imagine the one than the other. Nor need we fear that falsity may exist in the will or affections; for, although I may desire objects that are wrong, and even that never existed, it is still true that I desire them. There thus only remain our judgments, in which we must take diligent heed that we be not deceived. But the chief and most ordinary error that arises in them consists in judging that the ideas which are in us are like or conformed to the things that are external to us; for assuredly, if we but considered the ideas themselves as certain modes of our thought (consciousness), without referring them to anything beyond, they would hardly afford any occasion of error.

7. But among these ideas, some appear to me to be innate, others adventitious, and others to be made by myself (factitious); for, as I have the power of conceiving what is called a thing, or a truth, or a thought, it seems to me that I hold this power from no other source than my own nature; but if I now hear a noise, if I see the sun, or if I feel heat, I have all along judged that these sensations proceeded from certain objects existing out of myself; and, in fine, it appears to me that sirens, hippogryphs, and the like, are inventions of my own mind. But I may even perhaps come to be of opinion that all my ideas are of the class which I call adventitious, or that they are all innate, or that they are all factitious; for I have not yet clearly discovered their true origin.

8. What I have here principally to do is to consider, with reference to those that appear to come from certain objects without me, what grounds there are for thinking them like these

objects. The first of these grounds is that it seems to me I am so taught by nature; and the second that I am conscious that those ideas are not dependent on my will, and therefore not on myself, for they are frequently presented to me against my will, as at present, whether I will or not, I feel heat; and I am thus persuaded that this sensation or idea (sensum vel ideam) of heat is produced in me by something different from myself, viz., by the heat of the fire by which I sit. And it is very reasonable to suppose that this object impresses me with its own likeness rather than any other thing.

9. But I must consider whether these reasons are sufficiently strong and convincing. When I speak of being taught by nature in this matter, I understand by the word nature only a certain spontaneous impetus that impels me to believe in a resemblance between ideas and their objects, and not a natural light that affords a knowledge of its truth. But these two things are widely different; for what the natural light shows to be true can be in no degree doubtful, as, for example, that I am because I doubt, and other truths of the like kind; inasmuch as I possess no other faculty whereby to distinguish truth from error, which can teach me the falsity of what the natural light declares to be true, and which is equally trustworthy; but with respect to seemingly natural impulses, I have observed, when the question related to the choice of right or wrong in action, that they frequently led me to take the worse part; nor do I see that I have any better ground for following them in what relates to truth and error.

10. Then, with respect to the other reason, which is that because these ideas do not depend on my will, they must arise from objects existing without me, I do not find it more convincing than the former, for just as those natural impulses, of which I have lately spoken, are found in me, notwithstanding that they are not always in harmony with my will, so likewise it may

be that I possess some power not sufficiently known to myself capable of producing ideas without the aid of external objects, and, indeed, it has always hitherto appeared to me that they are formed during sleep, by some power of this nature, without the aid of aught external.

11. And, in fine, although I should grant that they proceeded from those objects, it is not a necessary consequence that they must be like them. On the contrary, I have observed, in a number of instances, that there was a great difference between the object and its idea. Thus, for example, I find in my mind two wholly diverse ideas of the sun; the one, by which it appears to me extremely small draws its origin from the senses, and should be placed in the class of adventitious ideas; the other, by which it seems to be many times larger than the whole earth, is taken up on astronomical grounds, that is, elicited from certain notions born with me, or is framed by myself in some other manner. These two ideas cannot certainly both resemble the same sun; and reason teaches me that the one which seems to have immediately emanated from it is the most unlike.

12. And these things sufficiently prove that hitherto it has not been from a certain and deliberate judgment, but only from a sort of blind impulse, that I believed existence of certain things different from myself, which, by the organs of sense, or by whatever other means it might be, conveyed their ideas or images into my mind and impressed it with their likenesses.

13. But there is still another way of inquiring whether, of the objects whose ideas are in my mind, there are any that exist out of me. If ideas are taken in so far only as they are certain modes of consciousness, I do not remark any difference or inequality among them, and all seem, in the same manner, to proceed from myself; but, considering them as images, of which one represents one thing and another a different, it is evident that a great

diversity obtains among them. For, without doubt, those that represent substances are something more, and contain in themselves, so to speak, more objective reality that is, participate by representation in higher degrees of being or perfection, than those that represent only modes or accidents; and again, the idea by which I conceive a God sovereign, eternal, infinite, immutable, all-knowing, all-powerful, and the creator of all things that are out of himself, this, I say, has certainly in it more objective reality than those ideas by which finite substances are represented.

14. Now, it is manifest by the natural light that there must at least be as much reality in the efficient and total cause as in its effect; for whence can the effect draw its reality if not from its cause ? And how could the cause communicate to it this reality unless it possessed it in itself? And hence it follows, not only that what is cannot be produced by what is not, but likewise that the more perfect, in other words, that which contains in itself more reality, cannot be the effect of the less perfect; and this is not only evidently true of those effects, whose reality is actual or formal, but likewise of ideas, whose reality is only considered as objective. Thus, for example, the stone that is not yet in existence, not only cannot now commence to be, unless it be produced by that which possesses in itself, formally or eminently, all that enters into its composition, in other words, by that which contains in itself the same properties that are in the stone, or others superior to them; and heat can only be produced in a subject that was before devoid of it, by a cause that is of an order, degree or kind, at least as perfect as heat; and so of the others. But further, even the idea of the heat, or of the stone, cannot exist in me unless it be put there by a cause that contains, at least, as much reality as I conceive existent in the heat or in the stone for although that cause may not transmit into my idea anything of its actual or formal reality, we ought not on this account to imagine that it is less real; but we

ought to consider that, as every idea is a work of the mind, its nature is such as of itself to demand no other formal reality than that which it borrows from our consciousness, of which it is but a mode that is, a manner or way of thinking. But in order that an idea may contain this objective reality rather than that, it must doubtless derive it from some cause in which is found at least as much formal reality as the idea contains of objective; for, if we suppose that there is found in an idea anything which was not in its cause, it must of course derive this from nothing. But, however imperfect may be the mode of existence by which a thing is objectively or by representation in the understanding by its idea, we certainly cannot, for all that, allege that this mode of existence is nothing, nor, consequently, that the idea owes its origin to nothing.

15. Nor must it be imagined that, since the reality which considered in these ideas is only objective, the same reality need not be formally (actually) in the causes of these ideas, but only objectively: for, just as the mode of existing objectively belongs to ideas by their peculiar nature, so likewise the mode of existing formally appertains to the causes of these ideas (at least to the first and principal), by their peculiar nature. And although an idea may give rise to another idea, this regress cannot, nevertheless, be infinite; we must in the end reach a first idea, the cause of which is, as it were, the archetype in which all the reality or perfection that is found objectively or by representation in these ideas is contained formally and in act. I am thus clearly taught by the natural light that ideas exist in me as pictures or images, which may, in truth, readily fall short of the perfection of the objects from which they are taken, but can never contain anything greater or more perfect.

16. And in proportion to the time and care with which I examine all those matters, the conviction of their truth brightens

and becomes distinct. But, to sum up, what conclusion shall I draw from it all? It is this: if the objective reality or perfection of any one of my ideas be such as clearly to convince me, that this same reality exists in me neither formally nor eminently, and if, as follows from this, I myself cannot be the cause of it, it is a necessary consequence that I am not alone in the world, but that there is besides myself some other being who exists as the cause of that idea; while, on the contrary, if no such idea be found in my mind, I shall have no sufficient ground of assurance of the existence of any other being besides myself, for, after a most careful search, I have, up to this moment, been unable to discover any other ground.

17. But, among these my ideas, besides that which represents myself, respecting which there can be here no difficulty, there is one that represents a God; others that represent corporeal and inanimate things; others angels; others animals; and, finally, there are some that represent men like myself.

18. But with respect to the ideas that represent other men, or animals, or angels, I can easily suppose that they were formed by the mingling and composition of the other ideas which I have of myself, of corporeal things, and of God, although they were, apart from myself, neither men, animals, nor angels.

19. And with regard to the ideas of corporeal objects, I never discovered in them anything so great or excellent which I myself did not appear capable of originating; for, by considering these ideas closely and scrutinizing them individually, in the same way that I yesterday examined the idea of wax, I find that there is but little in them that is clearly and distinctly perceived. As belonging to the class of things that are clearly apprehended, I recognize the following, viz, magnitude or extension in length, breadth, and depth; figure, which results from the termination of extension; situation, which bodies of diverse figures preserve with reference

to each other; and motion or the change of situation; to which may be added substance, duration, and number. But with regard to light, colors, sounds, odors, tastes, heat, cold, and the other tactile qualities, they are thought with so much obscurity and confusion, that I cannot determine even whether they are true or false; in other words, whether or not the ideas I have of these qualities are in truth the ideas of real objects. For although I before remarked that it is only in judgments that formal falsity, or falsity properly so called, can be met with, there may nevertheless be found in ideas a certain material falsity, which arises when they represent what is nothing as if it were something. Thus, for example, the ideas I have of cold and heat are so far from being clear and distinct, that I am unable from them to discover whether cold is only the privation of heat, or heat the privation of cold; or whether they are or are not real qualities: and since, ideas being as it were images there can be none that does not seem to us to represent some object, the idea which represents cold as something real and positive will not improperly be called false, if it be correct to say that cold is nothing but a privation of heat; and so in other cases.

20. To ideas of this kind, indeed, it is not necessary that I should assign any author besides myself: for if they are false, that is, represent objects that are unreal, the natural light teaches me that they proceed from nothing; in other words, that they are in me only because something is wanting to the perfection of my nature; but if these ideas are true, yet because they exhibit to me so little reality that I cannot even distinguish the object represented from nonbeing, I do not see why I should not be the author of them.

21. With reference to those ideas of corporeal things that are clear and distinct, there are some which, as appears to me, might have been taken from the idea I have of myself, as those of

substance, duration, number, and the like. For when I think that a stone is a substance, or a thing capable of existing of itself, and that I am likewise a substance, although I conceive that I am a thinking and non-extended thing, and that the stone, on the contrary, is extended and unconscious, there being thus the greatest diversity between the two concepts, yet these two ideas seem to have this in common that they both represent substances. In the same way, when I think of myself as now existing, and recollect besides that I existed some time ago, and when I am conscious of various thoughts whose number I know, I then acquire the ideas of duration and number, which I can afterward transfer to as many objects as I please. With respect to the other qualities that go to make up the ideas of corporeal objects, viz, extension, figure, situation, and motion, it is true that they are not formally in me, since I am merely a thinking being; but because they are only certain modes of substance, and because I myself am a substance, it seems possible that they may be contained in me eminently.

22. There only remains, therefore, the idea of God, in which I must consider whether there is anything that cannot be supposed to originate with myself. By the name God, I understand a substance infinite, eternal, immutable, independent, all-knowing, all-powerful, and by which I myself, and every other thing that exists, if any such there be, were created. But these properties are so great and excellent, that the more attentively I consider them the less I feel persuaded that the idea I have of them owes its origin to myself alone. And thus it is absolutely necessary to conclude, from all that I have before said, that God exists.

23. For though the idea of substance be in my mind owing to this, that I myself am a substance, I should not, however, have

the idea of an infinite substance, seeing I am a finite being, unless it were given me by some substance in reality infinite.

24. And I must not imagine that I do not apprehend the infinite by a true idea, but only by the negation of the finite, in the same way that I comprehend repose and darkness by the negation of motion and light: since, on the contrary, I clearly perceive that there is more reality in the infinite substance than in the finite, and therefore that in some way I possess the perception (notion) of the infinite before that of the finite, that is, the perception of God before that of myself, for how could I know that I doubt, desire, or that something is wanting to me, and that I am not wholly perfect, if I possessed no idea of a being more perfect than myself, by comparison of which I knew the deficiencies of my nature?

25. And it cannot be said that this idea of God is perhaps materially false, and consequently that it may have arisen from nothing in other words, that it may exist in me from my imperfections as I before said of the ideas of heat and cold, and the like: for, on the contrary, as this idea is very clear and distinct, and contains in itself more objective reality than any other, there can be no one of itself more true, or less open to the suspicion of falsity. The idea, I say, of a being supremely perfect, and infinite, is in the highest degree true; for although, perhaps, we may imagine that such a being does not exist, we cannot, nevertheless, suppose that his idea represents nothing real, as I have already said of the idea of cold. It is likewise clear and distinct in the highest degree, since whatever the mind clearly and distinctly conceives as real or true, and as implying any perfection, is contained entire in this idea. And this is true, nevertheless, although I do not comprehend the infinite, and although there may be in God an infinity of things that I cannot comprehend, nor perhaps even compass by thought in any way; for it is of the

nature of the infinite that it should not be comprehended by the finite; and it is enough that I rightly understand this, and judge that all which I clearly perceive, and in which I know there is some perfection, and perhaps also an infinity of properties of which I am ignorant, are formally or eminently in God, in order that the idea I have of him may be come the most true, clear, and distinct of all the ideas in my mind.

26. But perhaps I am something more than I suppose myself to be, and it may be that all those perfections which I attribute to God, in some way exist potentially in me, although they do not yet show themselves, and are not reduced to act. Indeed, I am already conscious that my knowledge is being increased and perfected by degrees; and I see nothing to prevent it from thus gradually increasing to infinity, nor any reason why, after such increase and perfection, I should not be able thereby to acquire all the other perfections of the Divine nature; nor, in fine, why the power I possess of acquiring those perfections, if it really now exist in me, should not be sufficient to produce the ideas of them.

27. Yet, on looking more closely into the matter, I discover that this cannot be; for, in the first place, although it were true that my knowledge daily acquired new degrees of perfection, and although there were potentially in my nature much that was not as yet actually in it, still all these excellences make not the slightest approach to the idea I have of the Deity, in whom there is no perfection merely potentially but all actually existent; for it is even an unmistakable token of imperfection in my knowledge, that it is augmented by degrees. Further, although my knowledge increase more and more, nevertheless I am not, therefore, induced to think that it will ever be actually infinite, since it can never reach that point beyond which it shall be incapable of further increase. But I conceive God as actually infinite, so that nothing can be added to his perfection. And, in fine, I readily perceive that the objective

being of an idea cannot be produced by a being that is merely potentially existent, which, properly speaking, is nothing, but only by a being existing formally or actually.

28. And, truly, I see nothing in all that I have now said which it is not easy for any one, who shall carefully consider it, to discern by the natural light; but when I allow my attention in some degree to relax, the vision of my mind being obscured, and, as it were, blinded by the images of sensible objects, I do not readily remember the reason why the idea of a being more perfect than myself, must of necessity have proceeded from a being in reality more perfect. On this account I am here desirous to inquire further, whether I, who possess this idea of God, could exist supposing there were no God.

29. And I ask, from whom could I, in that case, derive my existence? Perhaps from myself, or from my parents, or from some other causes less perfect than God; for anything more perfect, or even equal to God, cannot be thought or imagined.

30. But if I were independent of every other existence, and were myself the author of my being, I should doubt of nothing, I should desire nothing, and, in fine, no perfection would be awanting to me; for I should have bestowed upon myself every perfection of which I possess the idea, and I should thus be God. And it must not be imagined that what is now wanting to me is perhaps of more difficult acquisition than that of which I am already possessed; for, on the contrary, it is quite manifest that it was a matter of much higher difficulty that I, a thinking being, should arise from nothing, than it would be for me to acquire the knowledge of many things of which I am ignorant, and which are merely the accidents of a thinking substance; and certainly, if I possessed of myself the greater perfection of which I have now spoken in other words, if I were the author of my own existence, I would not at least have denied to myself things that may be more

easily obtained as that infinite variety of knowledge of which I am at present destitute. I could not, indeed, have denied to myself any property which I perceive is contained in the idea of God, because there is none of these that seems to me to be more difficult to make or acquire; and if there were any that should happen to be more difficult to acquire, they would certainly appear so to me (supposing that I myself were the source of the other things I possess), because I should discover in them a limit to my power.

31. And though I were to suppose that I always was as I now am, I should not, on this ground, escape the force of these reasonings, since it would not follow, even on this supposition, that no author of my existence needed to be sought after. For the whole time of my life may be divided into an infinity of parts, each of which is in no way dependent on any other; and, accordingly, because I was in existence a short time ago, it does not follow that I must now exist, unless in this moment some cause create me anew as it were, that is, conserve me. In truth, it is perfectly clear and evident to all who will attentively consider the nature of duration, that the conservation of a substance, in each moment of its duration, requires the same power and act that would be necessary to create it, supposing it were not yet in existence; so that it is manifestly a dictate of the natural light that conservation and creation differ merely in respect of our mode of thinking and not in reality.

32. All that is here required, therefore, is that I interrogate myself to discover whether I possess any power by means of which I can bring it about that I, who now am, shall exist a moment afterward: for, since I am merely a thinking thing (or since, at least, the precise question, in the meantime, is only of that part of myself), if such a power resided in me, I should, without doubt, be conscious of it; but I am conscious of no such

power, and thereby I manifestly know that I am dependent upon some being different from myself.

33. But perhaps the being upon whom I am dependent is not God, and I have been produced either by my parents, or by some causes less perfect than Deity. This cannot be: for, as I before said, it is perfectly evident that there must at least be as much reality in the cause as in its effect; and accordingly, since I am a thinking thing and possess in myself an idea of God, whatever in the end be the cause of my existence, it must of necessity be admitted that it is likewise a thinking being, and that it possesses in itself the idea and all the perfections I attribute to Deity. Then it may again be inquired whether this cause owes its origin and existence to itself, or to some other cause. For if it be self-existent, it follows, from what I have before laid down, that this cause is God; for, since it possesses the perfection of self-existence, it must likewise, without doubt, have the power of actually possessing every perfection of which it has the idea--in other words, all the perfections I conceive to belong to God. But if it owe its existence to another cause than itself, we demand again, for a similar reason, whether this second cause exists of itself or through some other, until, from stage to stage, we at length arrive at an ultimate cause, which will be God.

34. And it is quite manifest that in this matter there can be no infinite regress of causes, seeing that the question raised respects not so much the cause which once produced me, as that by which I am at this present moment conserved.

35. Nor can it be supposed that several causes concurred in my production, and that from one I received the idea of one of the perfections I attribute to Deity, and from another the idea of some other, and thus that all those perfections are indeed found somewhere in the universe, but do not all exist together in a single being who is God; for, on the contrary, the unity, the simplicity,

or inseparability of all the properties of Deity, is one of the chief perfections I conceive him to possess; and the idea of this unity of all the perfections of Deity could certainly not be put into my mind by any cause from which I did not likewise receive the ideas of all the other perfections; for no power could enable me to embrace them in an inseparable unity, without at the same time giving me the knowledge of what they were and of their existence in a particular mode.

36. Finally, with regard to my parents from whom it appears I sprung , although all that I believed respecting them be true, it does not, nevertheless, follow that I am conserved by them, or even that I was produced by them, in so far as I am a thinking being. All that, at the most, they contributed to my origin was the giving of certain dispositions (modifications) to the matter in which I have hitherto judged that I or my mind, which is what alone I now consider to be myself, is inclosed; and thus there can here be no difficulty with respect to them, and it is absolutely necessary to conclude from this alone that I am, and possess the idea of a being absolutely perfect, that is, of God, that his existence is most clearly demonstrated.

37. There remains only the inquiry as to the way in which I received this idea from God; for I have not drawn it from the senses, nor is it even presented to me unexpectedly, as is usual with the ideas of sensible objects, when these are presented or appear to be presented to the external organs of the senses; it is not even a pure production or fiction of my mind, for it is not in my power to take from or add to it; and consequently there but remains the alternative that it is innate, in the same way as is the idea of myself.

38. And, in truth, it is not to be wondered at that God, at my creation, implanted this idea in me, that it might serve, as it were, for the mark of the workman impressed on his work; and it

is not also necessary that the mark should be something different from the work itself; but considering only that God is my creator, it is highly probable that he in some way fashioned me after his own image and likeness, and that I perceive this likeness, in which is contained the idea of God, by the same faculty by which I apprehend myself, in other words, when I make myself the object of reflection, I not only find that I am an incomplete, imperfect and dependent being, and one who unceasingly aspires after something better and greater than he is; but, at the same time, I am assured likewise that he upon whom I am dependent possesses in himself all the goods after which I aspire and the ideas of which I find in my mind, and that not merely indefinitely and potentially, but infinitely and actually, and that he is thus God. And the whole force of the argument of which I have here availed myself to establish the existence of God, consists in this, that I perceive I could not possibly be of such a nature as I am, and yet have in my mind the idea of a God, if God did not in reality exist--this same God, I say, whose idea is in my mind--that is, a being who possesses all those lofty perfections, of which the mind may have some slight conception, without, however, being able fully to comprehend them, and who is wholly superior to all defect and has nothing that marks imperfection: whence it is sufficiently manifest that he cannot be a deceiver, since it is a dictate of the natural light that all fraud and deception spring from some defect.

39. But before I examine this with more attention, and pass on to the consideration of other truths that may be evolved out of it, I think it proper to remain here for some time in the contemplation of God himself--that I may ponder at leisure his marvelous attributes--and behold, admire, and adore the beauty of this light so unspeakably great, as far, at least, as the strength of my mind, which is to some degree dazzled by the sight, will

permit. For just as we learn by faith that the supreme felicity of another life consists in the contemplation of the Divine majesty alone, so even now we learn from experience that a like meditation, though incomparably less perfect, is the source of the highest satisfaction of which we are susceptible in this life.

MEDITATION IV
OF TRUTH AND ERROR

1. I HAVE been habituated these bygone days to detach my mind from the senses, and I have accurately observed that there is exceedingly little which is known with certainty respecting corporeal objects, that we know much more of the human mind, and still more of God himself. I am thus able now without difficulty to abstract my mind from the contemplation of sensible or imaginable objects, and apply it to those which, as disengaged from all matter, are purely intelligible. And certainly the idea I have of the human mind in so far as it is a thinking thing, and not extended in length, breadth, and depth, and participating in none of the properties of body, is incomparably more distinct than the idea of any corporeal object; and when I consider that I doubt, in other words, that I am an incomplete and dependent being, the idea of a complete and independent being, that is to say of God, occurs to my mind with so much clearness and distinctness, and from the fact alone that this idea is found in me, or that I who possess it exist, the conclusions that God exists, and that my own existence, each moment of its continuance, is absolutely dependent upon him, are so manifest, as to lead me to believe it impossible that the human mind can know anything with more clearness and certitude. And now I seem to discover a path that will conduct us from the contemplation of the true God, in whom are contained all the treasures of science and wisdom, to the knowledge of the other things in the universe.

2. For, in the first place, I discover that it is impossible for him ever to deceive me, for in all fraud and deceit there is a certain imperfection: and although it may seem that the ability to deceive is a mark of subtlety or power, yet the will testifies

without doubt of malice and weakness; and such, accordingly, cannot be found in God.

3. In the next place, I am conscious that I possess a certain faculty of judging or discerning truth from error, which I doubtless received from God, along with whatever else is mine; and since it is impossible that he should will to deceive me, it is likewise certain that he has not given me a faculty that will ever lead me into error, provided I use it aright.

4. And there would remain no doubt on this head, did it not seem to follow from this, that I can never therefore be deceived; for if all I possess be from God, and if he planted in me no faculty that is deceitful, it seems to follow that I can never fall into error. Accordingly, it is true that when I think only of God (when I look upon myself as coming from God, Fr.), and turn wholly to him, I discover in myself no cause of error or falsity: but immediately thereafter, recurring to myself, experience assures me that I am nevertheless subject to innumerable errors. When I come to inquire into the cause of these, I observe that there is not only present to my consciousness a real and positive idea of God, or of a being supremely perfect, but also, so to speak, a certain negative idea of nothing, in other words, of that which is at an infinite distance from every sort of perfection, and that I am, as it were, a mean between God and nothing, or placed in such a way between absolute existence and non-existence, that there is in truth nothing in me to lead me into error, in so far as an absolute being is my creator; but that, on the other hand, as I thus likewise participate in some degree of nothing or of nonbeing, in other words, as I am not myself the supreme Being, and as I am wanting in many perfections, it is not surprising I should fall into error. And I hence discern that error, so far as error is not something real, which depends for its existence on God, but is simply defect; and therefore that, in order to fall into it, it is not necessary God

should have given me a faculty expressly for this end, but that my being deceived arises from the circumstance that the power which God has given me of discerning truth from error is not infinite.

5. Nevertheless this is not yet quite satisfactory; for error is not a pure negation; in other words, it is not the simple deficiency or want of some knowledge which is not due, but the privation or want of some knowledge which it would seem I ought to possess. But, on considering the nature of God, it seems impossible that he should have planted in his creature any faculty not perfect in its kind, that is, wanting in some perfection due to it: for if it be true, that in proportion to the skill of the maker the perfection of his work is greater, what thing can have been produced by the supreme Creator of the universe that is not absolutely perfect in all its parts? And assuredly there is no doubt that God could have created me such as that I should never be deceived; it is certain, likewise, that he always wills what is best: is it better, then, that I should be capable of being deceived than that I should not ?

6. Considering this more attentively the first thing that occurs to me is the reflection that I must not be surprised if I am not always capable of comprehending the reasons why God acts as he does; nor must I doubt of his existence because I find, perhaps, that there are several other things besides the present respecting which I understand neither why nor how they were created by him; for, knowing already that my nature is extremely weak and limited, and that the nature of God, on the other hand, is immense, incomprehensible, and infinite, I have no longer any difficulty in discerning that there is an infinity of things in his power whose causes transcend the grasp of my mind: and this consideration alone is sufficient to convince me, that the whole class of final causes is of no avail in physical or natural things; for it appears to me that I cannot, without exposing myself to the

charge of temerity, seek to discover the impenetrable ends of Deity.

7. It further occurs to me that we must not consider only one creature apart from the others, if we wish to determine the perfection of the works of Deity, but generally all his creatures together; for the same object that might perhaps, with some show of reason, be deemed highly imperfect if it were alone in the world, may for all that be the most perfect possible, considered as forming part of the whole universe: and although, as it was my purpose to doubt of everything, I only as yet know with certainty my own existence and that of God, nevertheless, after having remarked the infinite power of Deity, I cannot deny that we may have produced many other objects, or at least that he is able to produce them, so that I may occupy a place in the relation of a part to the great whole of his creatures.

8. Whereupon, regarding myself more closely, and considering what my errors are (which alone testify to the existence of imperfection in me), I observe that these depend on the concurrence of two causes, viz, the faculty of cognition, which I possess, and that of election or the power of free choice,--in other words, the understanding and the will. For by the understanding alone, I neither affirm nor deny anything but merely apprehend (percipio) the ideas regarding which I may form a judgment; nor is any error, properly so called, found in it thus accurately taken. And although there are perhaps innumerable objects in the world of which I have no idea in my understanding, it cannot, on that account be said that I am deprived of those ideas as of something that is due to my nature, but simply that I do not possess them, because, in truth, there is no ground to prove that Deity ought to have endowed me with a larger faculty of cognition than he has actually bestowed upon me; and however skillful a workman I suppose him to be, I have

no reason, on that account, to think that it was obligatory on him to give to each of his works all the perfections he is able to bestow upon some. Nor, moreover, can I complain that God has not given me freedom of choice, or a will sufficiently ample and perfect, since, in truth, I am conscious of will so ample and extended as to be superior to all limits. And what appears to me here to be highly remarkable is that, of all the other properties I possess, there is none so great and perfect as that I do not clearly discern it could be still greater and more perfect. For, to take an example, if I consider the faculty of understanding which I possess, I find that it is of very small extent, and greatly limited, and at the same time I form the idea of another faculty of the same nature, much more ample and even infinite, and seeing that I can frame the idea of it, I discover, from this circumstance alone, that it pertains to the nature of God. In the same way, if I examine the faculty of memory or imagination, or any other faculty I possess, I find none that is not small and circumscribed, and in God immense and infinite. It is the faculty of will only, or freedom of choice, which I experience to be so great that I am unable to conceive the idea of another that shall be more ample and extended; so that it is chiefly my will which leads me to discern that I bear a certain image and similitude of Deity. For although the faculty of will is incomparably greater in God than in myself, as well in respect of the knowledge and power that are conjoined with it, and that render it stronger and more efficacious, as in respect of the object, since in him it extends to a greater number of things, it does not, nevertheless, appear to me greater, considered in itself formally and precisely: for the power of will consists only in this, that we are able to do or not to do the same thing (that is, to affirm or deny, to pursue or shun it), or rather in this alone, that in affirming or denying, pursuing or shunning, what is proposed to us by the understanding, we so act that we are not conscious of being determined to a particular action by any external force. For, to the possession of freedom, it is not necessary that I be alike indifferent toward each of two contraries; but, on the contrary, the more I am inclined toward the one, whether because I clearly know that in it there is the reason of truth and goodness, or because God thus internally disposes my thought, the more freely do I choose and embrace it; and assuredly divine grace and natural knowledge, very far from diminishing liberty, rather augment and fortify it. But the indifference of which I am conscious when I am not impelled to one side rather than to another for want of a reason, is the lowest grade of liberty, and manifests defect or negation of knowledge rather than perfection of will; for if I always clearly knew what was true and good, I should never have any difficulty in determining what judgment I ought to come to, and what choice I ought to make, and I should thus be entirely free without ever being indifferent.

9. From all this I discover, however, that neither the power of willing, which I have received from God, is of itself the source of my errors, for it is exceedingly ample and perfect in its kind; nor even the power of understanding, for as I conceive no object unless by means of the faculty that God bestowed upon me, all that I conceive is doubtless rightly conceived by me, and it is impossible for me to be deceived in it. Whence, then, spring my errors? They arise from this cause alone, that I do not restrain the will, which is of much wider range than the understanding, within the same limits, but extend it even to things I do not understand, and as the will is of itself indifferent to such, it readily falls into error and sin by choosing the false in room of the true, and evil instead of good.

10. For example, when I lately considered whether aught really existed in the world, and found that because I considered

this question, it very manifestly followed that I myself existed, I could not but judge that what I so clearly conceived was true, not that I was forced to this judgment by any external cause, but simply because great clearness of the understanding was succeeded by strong inclination in the will; and I believed this the more freely and spontaneously in proportion as I was less indifferent with respect to it. But now I not only know that I exist, in so far as I am a thinking being, but there is likewise presented to my mind a certain idea of corporeal nature; hence I am in doubt as to whether the thinking nature which is in me, or rather which I myself am, is different from that corporeal nature, or whether both are merely one and the same thing, and I here suppose that I am as yet ignorant of any reason that would determine me to adopt the one belief in preference to the other; whence it happens that it is a matter of perfect indifference to me which of the two suppositions I affirm or deny, or whether I form any judgment at all in the matter.

11. This indifference, moreover, extends not only to things of which the understanding has no knowledge at all, but in general also to all those which it does not discover with perfect clearness at the moment the will is deliberating upon them; for, however probable the conjectures may be that dispose me to form a judgment in a particular matter, the simple knowledge that these are merely conjectures, and not certain and indubitable reasons, is sufficient to lead me to form one that is directly the opposite. Of this I lately had abundant experience, when I laid aside as false all that I had before held for true, on the single ground that I could in some degree doubt of it.

12. But if I abstain from judging of a thing when I do not conceive it with sufficient clearness and distinctness, it is plain that I act rightly, and am not deceived; but if I resolve to deny or affirm, I then do not make a right use of my free will; and if I

affirm what is false, it is evident that I am deceived; moreover, even although I judge according to truth, I stumble upon it by chance, and do not therefore escape the imputation of a wrong use of my freedom; for it is a dictate of the natural light, that the knowledge of the understanding ought always to precede the determination of the will. And it is this wrong use of the freedom of the will in which is found the privation that constitutes the form of error. Privation, I say, is found in the act, in so far as it proceeds from myself, but it does not exist in the faculty which I received from God, nor even in the act, in so far as it depends on him.

13. For I have assuredly no reason to complain that God has not given me a greater power of intelligence or more perfect natural light than he has actually bestowed, since it is of the nature of a finite understanding not to comprehend many things, and of the nature of a created understanding to be finite; on the contrary, I have every reason to render thanks to God, who owed me nothing, for having given me all the perfections I possess, and I should be far from thinking that he has unjustly deprived me of, or kept back, the other perfections which he has not bestowed upon me.

14. I have no reason, moreover, to complain because he has given me a will more ample than my understanding, since, as the will consists only of a single element, and that indivisible, it would appear that this faculty is of such a nature that nothing could be taken from it without destroying it; and certainly, the more extensive it is, the more cause I have to thank the goodness of him who bestowed it upon me.

15. And, finally, I ought not also to complain that God concurs with me in forming the acts of this will, or the judgments in which I am deceived, because those acts are wholly true and good, in so far as they depend on God; and the ability to form

them is a higher degree of perfection in my nature than the want of it would be. With regard to privation, in which alone consists the formal reason of error and sin, this does not require the concurrence of Deity, because it is not a thing or existence, and if it be referred to God as to its cause, it ought not to be called privation, but negation according to the signification of these words in the schools. For in truth it is no imperfection in Deity that he has accorded to me the power of giving or withholding my assent from certain things of which he has not put a clear and distinct knowledge in my understanding; but it is doubtless an imperfection in me that I do not use my freedom aright, and readily give my judgment on matters which I only obscurely and confusedly conceive. I perceive, nevertheless, that it was easy for Deity so to have constituted me as that I should never be deceived, although I still remained free and possessed of a limited knowledge, viz., by implanting in my understanding a clear and distinct knowledge of all the objects respecting which I should ever have to deliberate; or simply by so deeply engraving on my memory the resolution to judge of nothing without previously possessing a clear and distinct conception of it, that I should never forget it. And I easily understand that, in so far as I consider myself as a single whole, without reference to any other being in the universe, I should have been much more perfect than I now am, had Deity created me superior to error; but I cannot therefore deny that it is not somehow a greater perfection in the universe, that certain of its parts are not exempt from defect, as others are, than if they were all perfectly alike. And I have no right to complain because God, who placed me in the world, was not willing that I should sustain that character which of all others is the chief and most perfect.

16. I have even good reason to remain satisfied on the ground that, if he has not given me the perfection of being

superior to error by the first means I have pointed out above, which depends on a clear and evident knowledge of all the matters regarding which I can deliberate, he has at least left in my power the other means, which is, firmly to retain the resolution never to judge where the truth is not clearly known to me: for, although I am conscious of the weakness of not being able to keep my mind continually fixed on the same thought, I can nevertheless, by attentive and oft-repeated meditation, impress it so strongly on my memory that I shall never fail to recollect it as often as I require it, and I can acquire in this way the habitude of not erring.

17. And since it is in being superior to error that the highest and chief perfection of man consists, I deem that I have not gained little by this day's meditation, in having discovered the source of error and falsity. And certainly this can be no other than what I have now explained: for as often as I so restrain my will within the limits of my knowledge, that it forms no judgment except regarding objects which are clearly and distinctly represented to it by the understanding, I can never be deceived; because every clear and distinct conception is doubtless something, and as such cannot owe its origin to nothing, but must of necessity have God for its author-- God, I say, who, as supremely perfect, cannot, without a contradiction, be the cause of any error; and consequently it is necessary to conclude that every such conception or judgment is true. Nor have I merely learned to-day what I must avoid to escape error, but also what I must do to arrive at the knowledge of truth; for I will assuredly reach truth if I only fix my attention sufficiently on all the things I conceive perfectly, and separate these from others which I conceive more confusedly and obscurely; to which for the future I shall give diligent heed.

MEDITATION V
OF THE ESSENCE OF MATERIAL THINGS; AND, AGAIN, OF GOD; THAT HE EXISTS

1. SEVERAL other questions remain for consideration respecting the attributes of God and my own nature or mind. I will, however, on some other occasion perhaps resume the investigation of these. Meanwhile, as I have discovered what must be done and what avoided to arrive at the knowledge of truth, what I have chiefly to do is to essay to emerge from the state of doubt in which I have for some time been, and to discover whether anything can be known with certainty regarding material objects.

2. But before considering whether such objects as I conceive exist without me, I must examine their ideas in so far as these are to be found in my consciousness, and discover which of them are distinct and which confused.

3. In the first place, I distinctly imagine that quantity which the philosophers commonly call continuous, or the extension in length, breadth, and depth that is in this quantity, or rather in the object to which it is attributed. Further, I can enumerate in it many diverse parts, and attribute to each of these all sorts of sizes, figures, situations, and local motions; and, in fine, I can assign to each of these motions all degrees of duration.

4. And I not only distinctly know these things when I thus consider them in general; but besides, by a little attention, I discover innumerable particulars respecting figures, numbers, motion, and the like, which are so evidently true, and so accordant with my nature, that when I now discover them I do not so much appear to learn anything new, as to call to remembrance what I before knew, or for the first time to remark

what was before in my mind, but to which I had not hitherto directed my attention.

5. And what I here find of most importance is, that I discover in my mind innumerable ideas of certain objects, which cannot be esteemed pure negations, although perhaps they possess no reality beyond my thought, and which are not framed by me though it may be in my power to think, or not to think them, but possess true and immutable natures of their own. As, for example, when I imagine a triangle, although there is not perhaps and never was in any place in the universe apart from my thought one such figure, it remains true nevertheless that this figure possesses a certain determinate nature, form, or essence, which is immutable and eternal, and not framed by me, nor in any degree dependent on my thought; as appears from the circumstance, that diverse properties of the triangle may be demonstrated, viz, that its three angles are equal to two right, that its greatest side is subtended by its greatest angle, and the like, which, whether I will or not, I now clearly discern to belong to it, although before I did not at all think of them, when, for the first time, I imagined a triangle, and which accordingly cannot be said to have been invented by me.

6. Nor is it a valid objection to allege, that perhaps this idea of a triangle came into my mind by the medium of the senses, through my having. seen bodies of a triangular figure; for I am able to form in thought an innumerable variety of figures with regard to which it cannot be supposed that they were ever objects of sense, and I can nevertheless demonstrate diverse properties of their nature no less than of the triangle, all of which are assuredly true since I clearly conceive them: and they are therefore something, and not mere negations; for it is highly evident that all that is true is something, truth being identical with existence; and I have already fully shown the truth of the principle, that whatever is clearly and distinctly known is true. And although this

had not been demonstrated, yet the nature of my mind is such as to compel me to assert to what I clearly conceive while I so conceive it; and I recollect that even when I still strongly adhered to the objects of sense, I reckoned among the number of the most certain truths those I clearly conceived relating to figures, numbers, and other matters that pertain to arithmetic and geometry, and in general to the pure mathematics.

7. But now if because I can draw from my thought the idea of an object, it follows that all I clearly and distinctly apprehend to pertain to this object, does in truth belong to it, may I not from this derive an argument for the existence of God? It is certain that I no less find the idea of a God in my consciousness, that is the idea of a being supremely perfect, than that of any figure or number whatever: and I know with not less clearness and distinctness that an actual and eternal existence pertains to his nature than that all which is demonstrable of any figure or number really belongs to the nature of that figure or number; and, therefore, although all the conclusions of the preceding Meditations were false, the existence of God would pass with me for a truth at least as certain as I ever judged any truth of mathematics to be.

8. Indeed such a doctrine may at first sight appear to contain more sophistry than truth. For, as I have been accustomed in every other matter to distinguish between existence and essence, I easily believe that the existence can be separated from the essence of God, and that thus God may be conceived as not actually existing. But, nevertheless, when I think of it more attentively, it appears that the existence can no more be separated from the essence of God, than the idea of a mountain from that of a valley, or the equality of its three angles to two right angles, from the essence of a rectilinear triangle; so that it is not less impossible to conceive a God, that is, a being supremely perfect, to whom

existence is awanting, or who is devoid of a certain perfection, than to conceive a mountain without a valley.

9. But though, in truth, I cannot conceive a God unless as existing, any more than I can a mountain without a valley, yet, just as it does not follow that there is any mountain in the world merely because I conceive a mountain with a valley, so likewise, though I conceive God as existing, it does not seem to follow on that account that God exists; for my thought imposes no necessity on things; and as I may imagine a winged horse, though there be none such, so I could perhaps attribute existence to God, though no God existed.

10. But the cases are not analogous, and a fallacy lurks under the semblance of this objection: for because I cannot conceive a mountain without a valley, it does not follow that there is any mountain or valley in existence, but simply that the mountain or valley, whether they do or do not exist, are inseparable from each other; whereas, on the other hand, because I cannot conceive God unless as existing, it follows that existence is inseparable from him, and therefore that he really exists: not that this is brought about by my thought, or that it imposes any necessity on things, but, on the contrary, the necessity which lies in the thing itself, that is, the necessity of the existence of God, determines me to think in this way: for it is not in my power to conceive a God without existence, that is, a being supremely perfect, and yet devoid of an absolute perfection, as I am free to imagine a horse with or without wings.

11. Nor must it be alleged here as an objection, that it is in truth necessary to admit that God exists, after having supposed him to possess all perfections, since existence is one of them, but that my original supposition was not necessary; just as it is not necessary to think that all quadrilateral figures can be inscribed in the circle, since, if I supposed this, I should be constrained to

admit that the rhombus, being a figure of four sides, can be therein inscribed, which, however, is manifestly false. This objection is, I say, incompetent; for although it may not be necessary that I shall at any time entertain the notion of Deity, yet each time I happen to think of a first and sovereign being, and to draw, so to speak, the idea of him from the storehouse of the mind, I am necessitated to attribute to him all kinds of perfections, though I may not then enumerate them all, nor think of each of them in particular. And this necessity is sufficient, as soon as I discover that existence is a perfection, to cause me to infer the existence of this first and sovereign being; just as it is not necessary that I should ever imagine any triangle, but whenever I am desirous of considering a rectilinear figure composed of only three angles, it is absolutely necessary to attribute those properties to it from which it is correctly inferred that its three angles are not greater than two right angles, although perhaps I may not then advert to this relation in particular. But when I consider what figures are capable of being inscribed in the circle, it is by no means necessary to hold that all quadrilateral figures are of this number; on the contrary, I cannot even imagine such to be the case, so long as I shall be unwilling to accept in thought aught that I do not clearly and distinctly conceive; and consequently there is a vast difference between false suppositions, as is the one in question, and the true ideas that were born with me, the first and chief of which is the idea of God. For indeed I discern on many grounds that this idea is not factitious depending simply on my thought, but that it is the representation of a true and immutable nature: in the first place because I can conceive no other being, except God, to whose essence existence necessarily pertains; in the second, because it is impossible to conceive two or more gods of this kind; and it being supposed that one such God exists, I clearly see that he must have existed from all eternity, and will exist to all eternity; and finally, because I apprehend many other properties in God, none of which I can either diminish or change.

12. But, indeed, whatever mode of probation I in the end adopt, it always returns to this, that it is only the things I clearly and distinctly conceive which have the power of completely persuading me. And although, of the objects I conceive in this manner, some, indeed, are obvious to every one, while others are only discovered after close and careful investigation; nevertheless after they are once discovered, the latter are not esteemed less certain than the former. Thus, for example, to take the case of a right-angled triangle, although it is not so manifest at first that the square of the base is equal to the squares of the other two sides, as that the base is opposite to the greatest angle; nevertheless, after it is once apprehended, we are as firmly persuaded of the truth of the former as of the latter. And, with respect to God if I were not pre-occupied by prejudices, and my thought beset on all sides by the continual presence of the images of sensible objects, I should know nothing sooner or more easily then the fact of his being. For is there any truth more clear than the existence of a Supreme Being, or of God, seeing it is to his essence alone that necessary and eterna existence pertains?

13. And although the right conception of this truth has cost me much close thinking, nevertheless at present I feel not only as assured of it as of what I deem most certain, but I remark further that the certitude of all other truths is so absolutely dependent on it that without this knowledge it is impossible ever to know anything perfectly.

14. For although I am of such a nature as to be unable, while I possess a very clear and distinct apprehension of a matter, to resist the conviction of its truth, yet because my constitution is also such as to incapacitate me from keeping my mind continually

fixed on the same object, and as I frequently recollect a past judgment without at the same time being able to recall the grounds of it, it may happen meanwhile that other reasons are presented to me which would readily cause me to change my opinion, if I did not know that God existed; and thus I should possess no true and certain knowledge, but merely vague and vacillating opinions. Thus, for example, when I consider the nature of the rectilinear triangle, it most clearly appears to me, who have been instructed in the principles of geometry, that its three angles are equal to two right angles, and I find it impossible to believe otherwise, while I apply my mind to the demonstration; but as soon as I cease from attending to the process of proof, although I still remember that I had a clear comprehension of it, yet I may readily come to doubt of the truth demonstrated, if I do not know that there is a God: for I may persuade myself that I have been so constituted by nature as to be sometimes deceived, even in matters which I think I apprehend with the greatest evidence and certitude, especially when I recollect that I frequently considered many things to be true and certain which other reasons afterward constrained me to reckon as wholly false.

15. But after I have discovered that God exists, seeing I also at the same time observed that all things depend on him, and that he is no deceiver, and thence inferred that all which I clearly and distinctly perceive is of necessity true: although I no longer attend to the grounds of a judgment, no opposite reason can be alleged sufficient to lead me to doubt of its truth, provided only I remember that I once possessed a clear and distinct comprehension of it. My knowledge of it thus becomes true and certain. And this same knowledge extends likewise to whatever I remember to have formerly demonstrated, as the truths of geometry and the like: for what can be alleged against them to lead me to doubt of them? Will it be that my nature is such that I

may be frequently deceived? But I already know that I cannot be deceived in judgments of the grounds of which I possess a clear knowledge. Will it be that I formerly deemed things to be true and certain which I afterward discovered to be false? But I had no clear and distinct knowledge of any of those things, and, being as yet ignorant of the rule by which I am assured of the truth of a judgment, I was led to give my assent to them on grounds which I afterward discovered were less strong than at the time I imagined them to be. What further objection, then, is there? Will it be said that perhaps I am dreaming (an objection I lately myself raised), or that all the thoughts of which I am now conscious have no more truth than the reveries of my dreams? But although, in truth, I should be dreaming, the rule still holds that all which is clearly presented to my intellect is indisputably true.

16. And thus I very clearly see that the certitude and truth of all science depends on the knowledge alone of the true God, insomuch that, before I knew him, I could have no perfect knowledge of any other thing. And now that I know him, I possess the means of acquiring a perfect knowledge respecting innumerable matters, as well relative to God himself and other intellectual objects as to corporeal nature, in so far as it is the object of pure mathematics which do not consider whether it exists or not.

MEDITATION VI
OF THE EXISTENCE OF MATERIAL THINGS, AND OF THE REAL DISTINCTION BETWEEN THE MIND AND BODY OF MAN

1. THERE now only remains the inquiry as to whether material things exist. With regard to this question, I at least know with certainty that such things may exist, in as far as they

constitute the object of the pure mathematics, since, regarding them in this aspect, I can conceive them clearly and distinctly. For there can be no doubt that God possesses the power of producing all the objects I am able distinctly to conceive, and I never considered anything impossible to him, unless when I experienced a contradiction in the attempt to conceive it aright. Further, the faculty of imagination which I possess, and of which I am conscious that I make use when I apply myself to the consideration of material things, is sufficient to persuade me of their existence: for, when I attentively consider what imagination is, I find that it is simply a certain application of the cognitive faculty (facultas cognoscitiva) to a body which is immediately present to it, and which therefore exists.

2. And to render this quite clear, I remark, in the first place, the difference that subsists between imagination and pure intellection or conception. For example, when I imagine a triangle I not only conceive (intelligo) that it is a figure comprehended by three lines, but at the same time also I look upon (intueor) these three lines as present by the power and internal application of my mind (acie mentis), and this is what I call imagining. But if I desire to think of a chiliogon, I indeed rightly conceive that it is a figure composed of a thousand sides, as easily as I conceive that a triangle is a figure composed of only three sides; but I cannot imagine the thousand sides of a chiliogon as I do the three sides of a triangle, nor, so to speak, view them as present with the eyes of my mind. And although, in accordance with the habit I have of always imagining something when I think of corporeal things, it may happen that, in conceiving a chiliogon, I confusedly represent some figure to myself, yet it is quite evident that this is not a chiliogon, since it in no wise differs from that which I would represent to myself, if I were to think of a myriogon, or any other figure of many sides; nor would this representation be of any use

in discovering and unfolding the properties that constitute the difference between a chiliogon and other polygons. But if the question turns on a pentagon, it is quite true that I can conceive its figure, as well as that of a chiliogon, without the aid of imagination; but I can likewise imagine it by applying the attention of my mind to its five sides, and at the same time to the area which they contain. Thus I observe that a special effort of mind is necessary to the act of imagination, which is not required to conceiving or understanding (ad intelligendum); and this special exertion of mind clearly shows the difference between imagination and pure intellection (imaginatio et intellectio pura).

3. I remark, besides, that this power of imagination which I possess, in as far as it differs from the power of conceiving, is in no way necessary to my nature or essence, that is, to the essence of my mind; for although I did not possess it, I should still remain the same that I now am, from which it seems we may conclude that it depends on something different from the mind. And I easily understand that, if some body exists, with which my mind is so conjoined and united as to be able, as it were, to consider it when it chooses, it may thus imagine corporeal objects; so that this mode of thinking differs from pure intellection only in this respect, that the mind in conceiving turns in some way upon itself, and considers some one of the ideas it possesses within itself; but in imagining it turns toward the body, and contemplates in it some object conformed to the idea which it either of itself conceived or apprehended by sense. I easily understand, I say, that imagination may be thus formed, if it is true that there are bodies; and because I find no other obvious mode of explaining it, I thence, with probability, conjecture that they exist, but only with probability; and although I carefully examine all things, nevertheless I do not find that, from the

distinct idea of corporeal nature I have in my imagination, I can necessarily infer the existence of any body.

4. But I am accustomed to imagine many other objects besides that corporeal nature which is the object of the pure mathematics, as, for example, colors, sounds, tastes, pain, and the like, although with less distinctness; and, inasmuch as I perceive these objects much better by the senses, through the medium of which and of memory, they seem to have reached the imagination, I believe that, in order the more advantageously to examine them, it is proper I should at the same time examine what sense-perception is, and inquire whether from those ideas that are apprehended by this mode of thinking (consciousness), I cannot obtain a certain proof of the existence of corporeal objects.

5. And, in the first place, I will recall to my mind the things I have hitherto held as true, because perceived by the senses, and the foundations upon which my belief in their truth rested; I will, in the second place, examine the reasons that afterward constrained me to doubt of them; and, finally, I will consider what of them I ought now to believe.

6. Firstly, then, I perceived that I had a head, hands, feet and other members composing that body which I considered as part, or perhaps even as the whole, of myself. I perceived further, that that body was placed among many others, by which it was capable of being affected in diverse ways, both beneficial and hurtful; and what was beneficial I remarked by a certain sensation of pleasure, and what was hurtful by a sensation of pain. And besides this pleasure and pain, I was likewise conscious of hunger, thirst, and other appetites, as well as certain corporeal inclinations toward joy, sadness, anger, and similar passions. And, out of myself, besides the extension, figure, and motions of bodies, I likewise perceived in them hardness, heat, and the other tactile qualities, and, in addition, light, colors, odors, tastes, and sounds, the

variety of which gave me the means of distinguishing the sky, the earth, the sea, and generally all the other bodies, from one another. And certainly, considering the ideas of all these qualities, which were presented to my mind, and which alone I properly and immediately perceived, it was not without reason that I thought I perceived certain objects wholly different from my thought, namely, bodies from which those ideas proceeded; for I was conscious that the ideas were presented to me without my consent being required, so that I could not perceive any object, however desirous I might be, unless it were present to the organ of sense; and it was wholly out of my power not to perceive it when it was thus present. And because the ideas I perceived by the senses were much more lively and clear, and even, in their own way, more distinct than any of those I could of myself frame by meditation, or which I found impressed on my memory, it seemed that they could not have proceeded from myself, and must therefore have been caused in me by some other objects; and as of those objects I had no knowledge beyond what the ideas themselves gave me, nothing was so likely to occur to my mind as the supposition that the objects were similar to the ideas which they caused. And because I recollected also that I had formerly trusted to the senses, rather than to reason, and that the ideas which I myself formed were not so clear as those I perceived by sense, and that they were even for the most part composed of parts of the latter, I was readily persuaded that I had no idea in my intellect which had not formerly passed through the senses. Nor was I altogether wrong in likewise believing that that body which, by a special right, I called my own, pertained to me more properly and strictly than any of the others; for in truth, I could never be separated from it as from other bodies; I felt in it and on account of it all my appetites and affections, and in fine I was affected in its parts by pain and the titillation of pleasure, and not in the parts of the other bodies that were separated from it. But when I inquired into the reason why, from this I know not what sensation of pain, sadness of mind should follow, and why from the sensation of pleasure, joy should arise, or why this indescribable twitching of the stomach, which I call hunger, should put me in mind of taking food, and the parchedness of the throat of drink, and so in other cases, I was unable to give any explanation, unless that I was so taught by nature; for there is assuredly no affinity, at least none that I am able to comprehend, between this irritation of the stomach and the desire of food, any more than between the perception of an object that causes pain and the consciousness of sadness which springs from the perception. And in the same way it seemed to me that all the other judgments I had formed regarding the objects of sense, were dictates of nature; because I remarked that those judgments were formed in me, before I had leisure to weigh and consider the reasons that might constrain me to form them.

7. But, afterward, a wide experience by degrees sapped the faith I had reposed in my senses; for I frequently observed that towers, which at a distance seemed round, appeared square, when more closely viewed, and that colossal figures, raised on the summits of these towers, looked like small statues, when viewed from the bottom of them; and, in other instances without number, I also discovered error in judgments founded on the external senses; and not only in those founded on the external, but even in those that rested on the internal senses; for is there aught more internal than pain ? And yet I have sometimes been informed by parties whose arm or leg had been amputated, that they still occasionally seemed to feel pain in that part of the body which they had lost, --a circumstance that led me to think that I could not be quite certain even that any one of my members was affected when I felt pain in it. And to these grounds of doubt I

shortly afterward also added two others of very wide generality: the first of them was that I believed I never perceived anything when awake which I could not occasionally think I also perceived when asleep, and as I do not believe that the ideas I seem to perceive in my sleep proceed from objects external to me, I did not any more observe any ground for believing this of such as I seem to perceive when awake; the second was that since I was as yet ignorant of the author of my being or at least supposed myself to be so, I saw nothing to prevent my having been so constituted by nature as that I should be deceived even in matters that appeared to me to possess the greatest truth. And, with respect to the grounds on which I had before been persuaded of the existence of sensible objects, I had no great difficulty in finding suitable answers to them; for as nature seemed to incline me to many things from which reason made me averse, I thought that I ought not to confide much in its teachings. And although the perceptions of the senses were not dependent on my will, I did not think that I ought on that ground to conclude that they proceeded from things different from myself, since perhaps there might be found in me some faculty, though hitherto unknown to me, which produced them.

8. But now that I begin to know myself better, and to discover more clearly the author of my being, I do not, indeed, think that I ought rashly to admit all which the senses seem to teach, nor, on the other hand, is it my conviction that I ought to doubt in general of their teachings.

9. And, firstly, because I know that all which I clearly and distinctly conceive can be produced by God exactly as I conceive it, it is sufficient that I am able clearly and distinctly to conceive one thing apart from another, in order to be certain that the one is different from the other, seeing they may at least be made to exist separately, by the omnipotence of God; and it matters not by

what power this separation is made, in order to be compelled to judge them different; and, therefore, merely because I know with certitude that I exist, and because, in the meantime, I do not observe that aught necessarily belongs to my nature or essence beyond my being a thinking thing, I rightly conclude that my essence consists only in my being a thinking thing or a substance whose whole essence or nature is merely thinking. And although I may, or rather, as I will shortly say, although I certainly do possess a body with which I am very closely conjoined; nevertheless, because, on the one hand, I have a clear and distinct idea of myself, in as far as I am only a thinking and unextended thing, and as, on the other hand, I possess a distinct idea of body, in as far as it is only an extended and unthinking thing, it is certain that I, that is, my mind, by which I am what I am, is entirely and truly distinct from my body, and may exist without it.

10. Moreover, I find in myself diverse faculties of thinking that have each their special mode: for example, I find I possess the faculties of imagining and perceiving, without which I can indeed clearly and distinctly conceive myself as entire, but I cannot reciprocally conceive them without conceiving myself, that is to say, without an intelligent substance in which they reside, for in the notion we have of them, or to use the terms of the schools in their formal concept, they comprise some sort of intellection; whence I perceive that they are distinct from myself as modes are from things. I remark likewise certain other faculties, as the power of changing place, of assuming diverse figures, and the like, that cannot be conceived and cannot therefore exist, any more than the preceding, apart from a substance in which they inhere. It is very evident, however, that these faculties, if they really exist, must belong to some corporeal or extended substance, since in their clear and distinct concept there is contained some sort of

extension, but no intellection at all. Further, I cannot doubt but that there is in me a certain passive faculty of perception, that is, of receiving and taking knowledge of the ideas of sensible things; but this would be useless to me, if there did not also exist in me, or in some other thing, another active faculty capable of forming and producing those ideas. But this active faculty cannot be in me in as far as I am but a thinking thing, seeing that it does not presuppose thought, and also that those ideas are frequently produced in my mind without my contributing to it in any way, and even frequently contrary to my will. This faculty must therefore exist in some substance different from me, in which all the objective reality of the ideas that are produced by this faculty is contained formally or eminently, as I before remarked; and this substance is either a body, that is to say, a corporeal nature in which is contained formally and in effect all that is objectively and by representation in those ideas; or it is God himself, or some other creature, of a rank superior to body, in which the same is contained eminently. But as God is no deceiver, it is manifest that he does not of himself and immediately communicate those ideas to me, nor even by the intervention of any creature in which their objective reality is not formally, but only eminently, contained. For as he has given me no faculty whereby I can discover this to be the case, but, on the contrary, a very strong inclination to believe that those ideas arise from corporeal objects, I do not see how he could be vindicated from the charge of deceit, if in truth they proceeded from any other source, or were produced by other causes than corporeal things: and accordingly it must be concluded, that corporeal objects exist. Nevertheless, they are not perhaps exactly such as we perceive by the senses, for their comprehension by the senses is, in many instances, very obscure and confused; but it is at least necessary to admit that all which I clearly and distinctly conceive as in them, that is, generally speaking all that is comprehended in the object of speculative geometry, really exists external to me.

11. But with respect to other things which are either only particular, as, for example, that the sun is of such a size and figure, etc., or are conceived with less clearness and distinctness, as light, sound, pain, and the like, although they are highly dubious and uncertain, nevertheless on the ground alone that God is no deceiver, and that consequently he has permitted no falsity in my opinions which he has not likewise given me a faculty of correcting, I think I may with safety conclude that I possess in myself the means of arriving at the truth. And, in the first place, it cannot be doubted that in each of the dictates of nature there is some truth: for by nature, considered in general, I now understand nothing more than God himself, or the order and disposition established by God in created things; and by my nature in particular I understand the assemblage of all that God has given me.

12. But there is nothing which that nature teaches me more expressly or more sensibly than that I have a body which is ill affected when I feel pain, and stands in need of food and drink when I experience the sensations of hunger and thirst, etc. And therefore I ought not to doubt but that there is some truth in these informations.

13. Nature likewise teaches me by these sensations of pain, hunger, thirst, etc., that I am not only lodged in my body as a pilot in a vessel, but that I am besides so intimately conjoined, and as it were intermixed with it, that my mind and body compose a certain unity. For if this were not the case, I should not feel pain when my body is hurt, seeing I am merely a thinking thing, but should perceive the wound by the understanding alone, just as a pilot perceives by sight when any part of his vessel is damaged; and when my body has need of food or drink, I should

have a clear knowledge of this, and not be made aware of it by the confused sensations of hunger and thirst: for, in truth, all these sensations of hunger, thirst, pain, etc., are nothing more than certain confused modes of thinking, arising from the union and apparent fusion of mind and body.

14. Besides this, nature teaches me that my own body is surrounded by many other bodies, some of which I have to seek after, and others to shun. And indeed, as I perceive different sorts of colors, sounds, odors, tastes, heat, hardness, etc., I safely conclude that there are in the bodies from which the diverse perceptions of the senses proceed, certain varieties corresponding to them, although, perhaps, not in reality like them; and since, among these diverse perceptions of the senses, some are agreeable, and others disagreeable, there can be no doubt that my body, or rather my entire self, in as far as I am composed of body and mind, may be variously affected, both beneficially and hurtfully, by surrounding bodies.

15. But there are many other beliefs which though seemingly the teaching of nature, are not in reality so, but which obtained a place in my mind through a habit of judging inconsiderately of things. It may thus easily happen that such judgments shall contain error: thus, for example, the opinion I have that all space in which there is nothing to affect or make an impression on my senses is void: that in a hot body there is something in every respect similar to the idea of heat in my mind; that in a white or green body there is the same whiteness or greenness which I perceive; that in a bitter or sweet body there is the same taste, and so in other instances; that the stars, towers, and all distant bodies, are of the same size and figure as they appear to our eyes, etc. But that I may avoid everything like indistinctness of conception, I must accurately define what I properly understand by being taught by nature. For nature is here taken in a narrower sense than

when it signifies the sum of all the things which God has given me; seeing that in that meaning the notion comprehends much that belongs only to the mind to which I am not here to be understood as referring when I use the term nature; as, for example, the notion I have of the truth, that what is done cannot be undone, and all the other truths I discern by the natural light without the aid of the body; and seeing that it comprehends likewise much besides that belongs only to body, and is not here any more contained under the name nature, as the quality of heaviness, and the like, of which I do not speak, the term being reserved exclusively to designate the things which God has given to me as a being composed of mind and body. But nature, taking the term in the sense explained, teaches me to shun what causes in me the sensation of pain, and to pursue what affords me the sensation of pleasure, and other things of this sort; but I do not discover that it teaches me, in addition to this, from these diverse perceptions of the senses, to draw any conclusions respecting external objects without a previous careful and mature consideration of them by the mind: for it is, as appears to me, the office of the mind alone, and not of the composite whole of mind and body, to discern the truth in those matters. Thus, although the impression a star makes on my eye is not larger than that from the flame of a candle, I do not, nevertheless, experience any real or positive impulse determining me to believe that the star is not greater than the flame; the true account of the matter being merely that I have so judged from my youth without any rational ground. And, though on approaching the fire I feel heat, and even pain on approaching it too closely, I have, however, from this no ground for holding that something resembling the heat I feel is in the fire, any more than that there is something similar to the pain; all that I have ground for believing is, that there is something in it, whatever it may be, which excites in me those sensations of heat or pain. So also, although there are spaces in which I find nothing to excite and affect my senses, I must not therefore conclude that those spaces contain in them no body; for I see that in this, as in many other similar matters, I have been accustomed to pervert the order of nature, because these perceptions of the senses, although given me by nature merely to signify to my mind what things are beneficial and hurtful to the composite whole of which it is a part, and being sufficiently clear and distinct for that purpose, are nevertheless used by me as infallible rules by which to determine immediately the essence of the bodies that exist out of me, of which they can of course afford me only the most obscure and confused knowledge.

16. But I have already sufficiently considered how it happens that, notwithstanding the supreme goodness of God, there is falsity in my judgments. A difficulty, however, here presents itself, respecting the things which I am taught by nature must be pursued or avoided, and also respecting the internal sensations in which I seem to have occasionally detected error, and thus to be directly deceived by nature: thus, for example, I may be so deceived by the agreeable taste of some viand with which poison has been mixed, as to be induced to take the poison. In this case, however, nature may be excused, for it simply leads me to desire the viand for its agreeable taste, and not the poison, which is unknown to it; and thus we can infer nothing from this circumstance beyond that our nature is not omniscient; at which there is assuredly no ground for surprise, since, man being of a finite nature, his knowledge must likewise be of a limited perfection.

17. But we also not unfrequently err in that to which we are directly impelled by nature, as is the case with invalids who desire drink or food that would be hurtful to them. It will here, perhaps, be alleged that the reason why such persons are deceived is that

their nature is corrupted; but this leaves the difficulty untouched, for a sick man is not less really the creature of God than a man who is in full health; and therefore it is as repugnant to the goodness of God that the nature of the former should be deceitful as it is for that of the latter to be so. And as a clock, composed of wheels and counter weights, observes not the less accurately all the laws of nature when it is ill made, and points out the hours incorrectly, than when it satisfies the desire of the maker in every respect; so likewise if the body of man be considered as a kind of machine, so made up and composed of bones, nerves, muscles, veins, blood, and skin, that although there were in it no mind, it would still exhibit the same motions which it at present manifests involuntarily, and therefore without the aid of the mind, and simply by the dispositions of its organs, I easily discern that it would also be as natural for such a body, supposing it dropsical, for example, to experience the parchedness of the throat that is usually accompanied in the mind by the sensation of thirst, and to be disposed by this parchedness to move its nerves and its other parts in the way required for drinking, and thus increase its malady and do itself harm, as it is natural for it, when it is not indisposed to be stimulated to drink for its good by a similar cause; and although looking to the use for which a clock was destined by its maker, I may say that it is deflected from its proper nature when it incorrectly indicates the hours, and on the same principle, considering the machine of the human body as having been formed by God for the sake of the motions which it usually manifests, although I may likewise have ground for thinking that it does not follow the order of its nature when the throat is parched and drink does not tend to its preservation, nevertheless I yet plainly discern that this latter acceptation of the term nature is very different from the other: for this is nothing more than a certain denomination, depending entirely on my thought, and hence called extrinsic, by which I compare a sick man and an imperfectly constructed clock with the idea I have of a man in good health and a well made clock; while by the other acceptation of nature is understood something which is truly found in things, and therefore possessed of some truth.

18. But certainly, although in respect of a dropsical body, it is only by way of exterior denomination that we say its nature is corrupted, when, without requiring drink, the throat is parched; yet, in respect of the composite whole, that is, of the mind in its union with the body, it is not a pure denomination, but really an error of nature, for it to feel thirst when drink would be hurtful to it: and, accordingly, it still remains to be considered why it is that the goodness of God does not prevent the nature of man thus taken from being fallacious.

19. To commence this examination accordingly, I here remark, in the first place, that there is a vast difference between mind and body, in respect that body, from its nature, is always divisible, and that mind is entirely indivisible. For in truth, when I consider the mind, that is, when I consider myself in so far only as I am a thinking thing, I can distinguish in myself no parts, but I very clearly discern that I am somewhat absolutely one and entire; and although the whole mind seems to be united to the whole body, yet, when a foot, an arm, or any other part is cut off, I am conscious that nothing has been taken from my mind; nor can the faculties of willing, perceiving, conceiving, etc., properly be called its parts, for it is the same mind that is exercised all entire in willing, in perceiving, and in conceiving, etc. But quite the opposite holds in corporeal or extended things; for I cannot imagine any one of them how small soever it may be, which I cannot easily sunder in thought, and which, therefore, I do not know to be divisible. This would be sufficient to teach me that

the mind or soul of man is entirely different from the body, if I had not already been apprised of it on other grounds.

20. I remark, in the next place, that the mind does not immediately receive the impression from all the parts of the body, but only from the brain, or perhaps even from one small part of it, viz, that in which the common sense (senses communis) is said to be, which as often as it is affected in the same way gives rise to the same perception in the mind, although meanwhile the other parts of the body may be diversely disposed, as is proved by innumerable experiments, which it is unnecessary here to enumerate.

21. I remark, besides, that the nature of body is such that none of its parts can be moved by another part a little removed from the other, which cannot likewise be moved in the same way by any one of the parts that lie between those two, although the most remote part does not act at all. As, for example, in the cord A, B, C, D, which is in tension, if its last part D, be pulled, the first part A, will not be moved in a different way than it would be were one of the intermediate parts B or C to be pulled, and the last part D meanwhile to remain fixed. And in the same way, when I feel pain in the foot, the science of physics teaches me that this sensation is experienced by means of the nerves dispersed over the foot, which, extending like cords from it to the brain, when they are contracted in the foot, contract at the same time the inmost parts of the brain in which they have their origin, and excite in these parts a certain motion appointed by nature to cause in the mind a sensation of pain, as if existing in the foot; but as these nerves must pass through the tibia, the leg, the loins, the back, and neck, in order to reach the brain, it may happen that although their extremities in the foot are not affected, but only certain of their parts that pass through the loins or neck, the same movements, nevertheless, are excited in the brain by this motion

as would have been caused there by a hurt received in the foot, and hence the mind will necessarily feel pain in the foot, just as if it had been hurt; and the same is true of all the other perceptions of our senses.

22. I remark, finally, that as each of the movements that are made in the part of the brain by which the mind is immediately affected, impresses it with but a single sensation, the most likely supposition in the circumstances is, that this movement causes the mind to experience, among all the sensations which it is capable of impressing upon it; that one which is the best fitted, and generally the most useful for the preservation of the human body when it is in full health. But experience shows us that all the perceptions which nature has given us are of such a kind as I have mentioned; and accordingly, there is nothing found in them that does not manifest the power and goodness of God. Thus, for example, when the nerves of the foot are violently or more than usually shaken, the motion passing through the medulla of the spine to the innermost parts of the brain affords a sign to the mind on which it experiences a sensation, viz, of pain, as if it were in the foot, by which the mind is admonished and excited to do its utmost to remove the cause of it as dangerous and hurtful to the foot. It is true that God could have so constituted the nature of man as that the same motion in the brain would have informed the mind of something altogether different: the motion might, for example, have been the occasion on which the mind became conscious of itself, in so far as it is in the brain, or in so far as it is in some place intermediate between the foot and the brain, or, finally, the occasion on which it perceived some other object quite different, whatever that might be; but nothing of all this would have so well contributed to the preservation of the body as that which the mind actually feels. In the same way, when we stand in need of drink, there arises from this want a certain parchedness in

the throat that moves its nerves, and by means of them the internal parts of the brain; and this movement affects the mind with the sensation of thirst, because there is nothing on that occasion which is more useful for us than to be made aware that we have need of drink for the preservation of our health; and so in other instances.

23. Whence it is quite manifest that, notwithstanding the sovereign goodness of God, the nature of man, in so far as it is composed of mind and body, cannot but be sometimes fallacious. For, if there is any cause which excites, not in the foot, but in some one of the parts of the nerves that stretch from the foot to the brain, or even in the brain itself, the same movement that is ordinarily created when the foot is ill affected, pain will be felt, as it were, in the foot, and the sense will thus be naturally deceived; for as the same movement in the brain can but impress the mind with the same sensation, and as this sensation is much more frequently excited by a cause which hurts the foot than by one acting in a different quarter, it is reasonable that it should lead the mind to feel pain in the foot rather than in any other part of the body. And if it sometimes happens that the parchedness of the throat does not arise, as is usual, from drink being necessary for the health of the body, but from quite the opposite cause, as is the case with the dropsical, yet it is much better that it should be deceitful in that instance, than if, on the contrary, it were continually fallacious when the body is well-disposed; and the same holds true in other cases.

24. And certainly this consideration is of great service, not only in enabling me to recognize the errors to which my nature is liable, but likewise in rendering it more easy to avoid or correct them: for, knowing that all my senses more usually indicate to me what is true than what is false, in matters relating to the advantage of the body, and being able almost always to make use of more

than a single sense in examining the same object, and besides this, being able to use my memory in connecting present with past knowledge, and my understanding which has already discovered all the causes of my errors, I ought no longer to fear that falsity may be met with in what is daily presented to me by the senses. And I ought to reject all the doubts of those bygone days, as hyperbolical and ridiculous, especially the general uncertainty respecting sleep, which I could not distinguish from the waking state: for I now find a very marked difference between the two states, in respect that our memory can never connect our dreams with each other and with the course of life, in the way it is in the habit of doing with events that occur when we are awake. And, in truth, if some one, when I am awake, appeared to me all of a sudden and as suddenly disappeared, as do the images I see in sleep, so that I could not observe either whence he came or whither he went, I should not without reason esteem it either a specter or phantom formed in my brain, rather than a real man. But when I perceive objects with regard to which I can distinctly determine both the place whence they come, and that in which they are, and the time at which they appear to me, and when, without interruption, I can connect the perception I have of them with the whole of the other parts of my life, I am perfectly sure that what I thus perceive occurs while I am awake and not during sleep. And I ought not in the least degree to doubt of the truth of these presentations, if, after having called together all my senses, my memory, and my understanding for the purpose of examining them, no deliverance is given by any one of these faculties which is repugnant to that of any other: for since God is no deceiver, it necessarily follows that I am not herein deceived. But because the necessities of action frequently oblige us to come to a determination before we have had leisure for so careful an examination, it must be confessed that the life of man is frequently obnoxious to error with respect to individual objects; and we must, in conclusion, acknowledge the weakness of our nature.

SELECTIONS FROM THE PRINCIPLES OF PHILOSOPHY

OF

Rene Descartes

Translated by John Veitch

From the Publisher's Preface.

The present volume contains a reprint of the preface and the first part of the Principles of Philosophy, together with selections from the second, third and fourth parts of that work, corresponding to the extracts in the French edition of Garnier, are also given, as well as an appendix containing part of Descartes' reply to the Second Objections (viz., his formal demonstrations of the existence of Deity). The translation is based on the original Latin edition of the Principles, published in 1644.

The work had been translated into French during Descartes' lifetime, and personally revised and corrected by him, the French text is evidently deserving of the same consideration as the Latin originals, and consequently, the additions and variations of the French version have also been given—the additions being put in square brackets in the text and the variations in the footnotes.

LETTER OF THE AUTHOR

TO THE FRENCH TRANSLATOR OF THE PRINCIPLES OF PHILOSOPHY SERVING FOR A PREFACE.

Sir,—The version of my principles which you have been at pains to make, is so elegant and finished as to lead me to expect that the work will be more generally read in French than in Latin, and better understood. The only apprehension I entertain is lest the title should deter some who have not been brought up to letters, or with whom philosophy is in bad repute, because the kind they were taught has proved unsatisfactory; and this makes me think that it will be useful to add a preface to it for the purpose of showing what the MATTER of the work is, what END I had in view in writing it, and what UTILITY may be derived from it. But although it might be my part to write a preface of this nature, seeing I ought to know those particulars better than any other person, I cannot nevertheless prevail upon myself to do anything more than merely to give a summary of the chief points that fall, as I think, to be discussed in it: and I leave it to your discretion to present to the public such part of them as you shall judge proper.

I should have desired, in the first place, to explain in it what philosophy is, by commencing with the most common matters, as, for example, that the word PHILOSOPHY signifies the study of wisdom, and that by wisdom is to be understood not merely prudence in the management of affairs, but a perfect knowledge of all that man can know, as well for the conduct of his life as for the preservation of his health and the discovery of all the arts, and that knowledge to subserve these ends must necessarily be deduced from first causes; so that in order to study the acquisition of it (which is properly called philosophizing), we must commence with the investigation of those first causes which are called PRINCIPLES. Now these principles must possess TWO CONDITIONS: in the first place, they must be so clear and evident that the human mind, when it attentively considers them, cannot doubt of their truth; in the second place, the knowledge of other things must be so dependent on them as that though the principles themselves may indeed be known apart from what depends on them, the latter cannot nevertheless be known apart from the former. It will accordingly be necessary thereafter to endeavour so to deduce from those principles the knowledge of the things that depend on them, as that there may be nothing in the whole series of deductions which is not perfectly manifest. God is in truth the only being who is absolutely wise, that is, who possesses a perfect knowledge of all things; but we may say that men are more or less wise as their knowledge of the most important truths is greater or less. And I am confident that there is nothing, in what I have now said, in which all the learned do not concur.

I should, in the next place, have proposed to consider the utility of philosophy, and at the same time have shown that, since it embraces all that the human mind can know, we ought to believe that it is by it we are distinguished from savages and barbarians, and that the civilisation and culture of a nation is regulated by the degree in which true philosophy nourishes in it, and, accordingly, that to contain true philosophers is the highest privilege a state can enjoy. Besides this, I should have shown that, as regards individuals, it is not only useful for each man to have intercourse with those who apply themselves to this study, but that it is incomparably better he should himself direct his attention to it; just as it is doubtless to be preferred that a man should make use of his own eyes to direct his steps, and enjoy by means of the same the beauties of colour and light, than that he should blindly follow the guidance of another; though the latter course is certainly better than to have the eyes closed with no guide except one's self. But to live without philosophizing is in truth the same as keeping the eyes closed without attempting to open them; and the pleasure of seeing all that sight discloses is not to be compared with the satisfaction afforded by the discoveries of philosophy. And, finally, this study is more imperatively requisite for the regulation of our manners, and for conducting us through life, than is the use of our eyes for directing our steps. The brutes, which have only their bodies to conserve, are continually occupied in seeking sources of nourishment; but men, of whom the chief part is the mind, ought to make the search after wisdom their principal care, for wisdom is the true nourishment of the mind; and I feel assured, moreover, that there are very many who would not fail in the search, if they would but hope for success in it, and knew the degree of their capabilities for it. There is no mind, how ignoble soever it be, which remains so firmly bound up in the objects of the senses, as not sometime or other to turn itself away from them in the aspiration after some higher good, although not knowing frequently wherein that good consists. The greatest favourites of fortune—those who have health, honours, and riches in abundance— are not more exempt from aspirations of this nature than others; nay, I am persuaded that these are the persons who sigh the most deeply after another good greater and more perfect still than any they already possess. But the supreme good, considered by natural reason without the light of faith, is nothing more than the knowledge of truth through its first causes, in other words, the wisdom of which philosophy is the study. And, as all these particulars are indisputably true, all that is required to gain assent to their truth is that they be well stated.

But as one is restrained from assenting to these doctrines by experience, which shows that they who make pretensions to philosophy are often less wise and reasonable than others who never applied themselves to the study, I should have here shortly explained wherein consists all the science we now possess, and what are the degrees of wisdom at which we have arrived. The first degree contains only notions so clear of themselves that they can be acquired without meditation; the second comprehends all that the experience of the senses dictates; the third, that which the conversation of other men teaches us; to which may be added as the fourth, the reading, not of all books, but especially of such as have been written by persons capable of conveying proper instruction, for it is a species of conversation we hold with their authors. And it seems to me that all the wisdom we in ordinary possess is acquired only in these four ways; for I do not class divine revelation among them, because it does not conduct us by degrees, but elevates us at once to an infallible faith.

There have been, indeed, in all ages great minds who endeavoured to find a fifth road to wisdom, incomparably more sure and elevated than the other four. The path they essayed was the search of first causes and true principles, from which might be deduced the reasons of all that can be known by man; and it is to them the appellation of philosophers has been more especially accorded. I am not aware that there is any one of them up to the present who has succeeded in this enterprise. The first and chief whose writings we possess are Plato and Aristotle, between whom there was no difference, except that the former, following in the footsteps of his master, Socrates, ingenuously confessed that he had never yet been able to find anything certain, and that he was contented to write what seemed to him probable, imagining, for this end, certain principles by which he endeavoured to account for the other things. Aristotle, on the other hand, characterised by less candour, although for twenty years the disciple of Plato, and with no principles beyond those of his master, completely reversed his mode of putting them, and proposed as true and certain what it is probable he himself never esteemed as such. But these two men had acquired much judgment and wisdom by the four preceding means, qualities which raised their authority very high, so much so that those who succeeded them were willing rather to acquiesce in their opinions, than to seek better for themselves. The chief question among their disciples, however, was as to whether we ought to doubt of all things or hold some as certain,—a dispute which led them on both sides into extravagant errors; for a part of those who were for doubt, extended it even to the actions of life, to the neglect of the most ordinary rules required for its conduct; those, on the other hand, who maintained the doctrine of certainty, supposing that it must depend upon the senses, trusted entirely to them. To such an extent was this carried by Epicurus, that it is said he ventured to affirm, contrary to all the reasonings of the astronomers, that the sun is no larger than it appears.

It is a fault we may remark in most disputes, that, as truth is the mean between the two opinions that are upheld, each disputant departs from it in proportion to the degree in which he possesses the spirit of contradiction. But the error of those who leant too much to the side of doubt, was not followed for any length of time, and that of the opposite party has been to some extent corrected by the doctrine that the senses are deceitful in many instances. Nevertheless, I do not know that this error was wholly removed by showing that certitude is not in the senses, but in the understanding alone when it has clear perceptions; and that while we only possess the knowledge which is acquired in the first four grades of wisdom, we ought not to doubt of the things that appear to be true in what regards the conduct of life, nor esteem them as so certain that we cannot change our opinions regarding them, even though constrained by the evidence of reason.

From ignorance of this truth, or, if there was any one to whom it was known, from neglect of it, the majority of those who in these later ages aspired to be philosophers, blindly followed Aristotle, so that they frequently corrupted the sense of his writings, and attributed to him various opinions which he would not recognise as his own were he now to return to the world; and those who did not follow him, among whom are to be found many of the greatest minds, did yet not escape being imbued with his opinions in their youth, as these form the staple of instruction in the schools; and thus their minds were so preoccupied that they could not rise to the knowledge of true principles. And though I hold all the philosophers in esteem, and am unwilling to incur odium by my censure, I can adduce a proof of my assertion, which I do not think any of them will gainsay, which is, that they all laid down as a principle what they did not perfectly know. For example, I know none of them who did not suppose that there was gravity in terrestrial bodies; but although experience shows us very clearly that bodies we call heavy descend towards the center of the earth, we do not, therefore, know the nature of gravity, that is, the cause or principle in virtue of which bodies descend, and we must derive our knowledge of it from some other source. The same may be said of a vacuum and atoms, of heat and cold, of dryness and humidity, and of salt, sulphur, and mercury, and the other things of this sort which some have adopted as their principles. But no conclusion deduced from a principle which is not clear can be evident, even although the deduction be formally valid; and hence it follows that no reasonings based on such principles could lead them to the certain knowledge of any one thing, nor consequently advance them one step in the search after wisdom. And if they did discover any truth, this was due to one or other of the four means above mentioned. Notwithstanding this, I am in no degree desirous to lessen the honour which each of them can justly claim; I am only constrained to say, for the consolation of those who have not given their attention to study, that just as in travelling, when we turn our back upon the place to which we were going, we recede the farther from it in proportion as we proceed in the new direction for a greater length of time and with greater speed, so that, though we may be afterwards brought back to the right way, we cannot nevertheless arrive at the destined place as soon as if we had not moved backwards at all; so in philosophy, when we make use of false principles, we depart the farther from the knowledge of truth and wisdom exactly in proportion to the care with which we cultivate them, and apply ourselves to the deduction of diverse consequences from them, thinking that we are philosophizing well, while we are only departing the farther from the truth; from which it must be inferred that they who have learned the least of all that has been hitherto distinguished by the name of philosophy are the most fitted for the apprehension of truth.

After making those matters clear, I should, in the next place, have desired to set forth the grounds for holding that the true principles by which we may reach that highest degree of wisdom wherein consists the sovereign good of human life, are those I have proposed in this work; and two considerations alone are sufficient to establish this—the first of which is, that these principles are very clear, and the second, that we can deduce all other truths from them; for it is only these two conditions that are required in true principles. But I easily prove that they are very clear; firstly, by a reference to the manner in which I found them, namely, by rejecting all propositions that were in the least doubtful, for it is certain that such as could not be rejected by this test when they were attentively considered, are the most evident and clear which the human mind can know. Thus by considering that he who strives to doubt of all is unable nevertheless to doubt that he is while he doubts, and that what reasons thus, in not being able to doubt of itself and doubting nevertheless of everything else, is not that which we call our body, but what we name our mind or thought, I have taken the existence of this thought for the first principle, from which I very clearly deduced the following truths, namely, that there is a God who is the author of all that is in the world, and who, being the source of all truth, cannot have created our understanding of such a nature as to be deceived in the judgments it forms of the things of which it possesses a very clear and distinct perception. Those are all the principles of which I avail myself touching immaterial or metaphysical objects, from which I most clearly deduce these other principles of physical or corporeal things, namely, that there are bodies extended in length, breadth, and depth, which are of diverse figures and are moved in a variety of ways. Such are in sum the principles from which I deduce all other truths. The second circumstance that proves the clearness of these principles is, that they have been known in all ages, and even received as true and indubitable by all men, with the exception only of the existence of God, which has been doubted by some, because they attributed too much to the perceptions of the senses, and God can neither be seen nor touched.

But, though all the truths which I class among my principles were known at all times, and by all men, nevertheless, there has been no one up to the present, who, so far as I know, has adopted them as principles of philosophy: in other words, as such that we can deduce from them the knowledge of whatever else is in the world. It accordingly now remains for me to prove that they are such; and it appears to me that I cannot better establish this than by the test of experience: in other words, by inviting readers to peruse the following work. For, though I have not treated in it of all matters- -that being impossible—I think I have so explained all of which I had occasion to treat, that they who read it attentively will have ground for the persuasion that it is unnecessary to seek for any other principles than those I have given, in order to arrive at the most exalted knowledge of which the mind of man is capable; especially if, after the perusal of my writings, they take the trouble to consider how many diverse questions are therein discussed and explained, and, referring to the writings of others, they see how little probability there is in the reasons that are adduced in explanation of the same questions by principles different from mine. And that they may the more easily undertake this, I might have said that those imbued with my doctrines have much less difficulty in comprehending the writings of others, and estimating their true value, than those who have not been so imbued; and this is precisely the opposite of what I before said of such as commenced with the ancient philosophy, namely, that the more they have studied it the less fit are they for rightly apprehending the truth.

I should also have added a word of advice regarding the manner of reading this work, which is, that I should wish the reader at first to go over the whole of it, as he would a romance, without greatly straining his attention, or tarrying at the difficulties he may perhaps meet with in it, with the view simply of knowing in general the matters of which I treat; and that afterwards, if they seem to him to merit a more careful examination, and he feel a desire to know their causes, he may read it a second time, in order to observe the connection of my reasonings; but that he must not then give it up in despair, although he may not everywhere sufficiently discover the connection of the proof, or understand all the reasonings—it being only necessary to mark with a pen the places where the difficulties occur, and continue to read without interruption to the end; then, if he does not grudge to take up the book a third time, I am confident he will find in a fresh perusal the solution of most of the difficulties he will have marked before; and that, if any still remain, their solution will in the end be found in another reading.

I have observed, on examining the natural constitutions of different minds, that there are hardly any so dull or slow of understanding as to be incapable of apprehending good opinions, or even of acquiring all the highest sciences, if they be but conducted along the right road. And this can also be proved by reason; for, as the principles are clear, and as nothing ought to be deduced from them, unless most manifest inferences, no one is so devoid of intelligence as to be unable to comprehend the conclusions that flow from them. But, besides the entanglement of prejudices, from which no one is entirely exempt, although it is they who have been the most ardent students of the false sciences that receive the greatest detriment from them, it happens very generally that people of ordinary capacity neglect to study from a conviction that they want ability, and that others, who are more ardent, press on too rapidly: whence it comes to pass that they frequently admit principles far from evident, and draw doubtful inferences from them. For this reason, I should wish to assure those who are too distrustful of their own ability that there is nothing in my writings which they may not entirely understand, if they only take the trouble to examine them; and I should wish, at the same time, to warn those of an opposite tendency that even the most superior minds will have need of much time and attention to remark all I designed to embrace therein.

After this, that I might lead men to understand the real design I had in publishing them, I should have wished here to explain the order which it seems to me one ought to follow with the view of instructing himself. In the first place, a man who has merely the vulgar and imperfect knowledge which can be acquired by the four means above explained, ought, before all else, to endeavour to form for himself a code of morals, sufficient to regulate the actions of his life, as well for the reason that this does not admit of delay as because it ought to be our first care to live well. In the next place, he ought to study Logic, not that of the schools, for it is only, properly speaking, a dialectic which teaches the mode of expounding to others what we already know, or even of speaking much, without judgment, of what we do not know, by which means it corrupts rather than increases good sense—but the logic which teaches the right conduct of the reason with the view of discovering the truths of which we are ignorant; and, because it greatly depends on usage, it is desirable he should exercise himself for a length of time in practising its rules on easy and simple questions, as those of the mathematics. Then, when he has acquired some skill in discovering the truth in these questions, he should commence to apply himself in earnest to true philosophy, of which the first part is Metaphysics, containing the principles of knowledge, among which is the explication of the principal attributes of God, of the immateriality of the soul, and of all the clear and simple notions that are in us; the second is Physics, in which, after finding the true principles of material things, we examine, in general, how the whole universe has been framed; in the next place, we consider, in particular, the nature of the earth, and of all the bodies that are most generally found upon it, as air, water, fire, the loadstone and other minerals. In the next place it is necessary also to examine singly the nature of plants, of animals, and above all of man, in order that we may thereafter be able to discover the other sciences that are useful to us. Thus, all Philosophy is like a tree, of which Metaphysics is the root, Physics the trunk, and all the other sciences the branches that grow out of this trunk, which are reduced to three principal, namely, Medicine, Mechanics, and Ethics. By the science of Morals, I understand the highest and most perfect which, presupposing an entire knowledge of the other sciences, is the last degree of wisdom.

But as it is not from the roots or the trunks of trees that we gather the fruit, but only from the extremities of their branches, so the principal utility of philosophy depends on the separate uses of its parts, which we can only learn last of all. But, though I am ignorant of almost all these, the zeal I have always felt in endeavouring to be of service to the public, was the reason why I published, some ten or twelve years ago, certain Essays on the doctrines I thought I had acquired. The first part of these Essays was a "Discourse on the Method of rightly conducting the Reason, and seeking Truth in the Sciences," in which I gave a summary of the principal rules of logic, and also of an imperfect ethic, which a person may follow provisionally so long as he does not know any better. The other parts were three treatises: the first of Dioptrics, the second of Meteors, and the third of Geometry. In the Dioptrics, I designed to show that we might proceed far enough in philosophy as to arrive, by its means, at the knowledge of the arts that are useful to life, because the invention of the telescope, of which I there gave an explanation, is one of the most difficult that has ever been made. In the treatise of Meteors, I desired to exhibit the difference that subsists between the philosophy I cultivate and that taught in the schools, in which the same matters are usually discussed. In fine, in the Geometry, I professed to demonstrate that I had discovered many things that were before unknown, and thus afford ground for believing that we may still discover many others, with the view of thus stimulating all to the investigation of truth. Since that period, anticipating the difficulty which many would experience in apprehending the foundations of the Metaphysics, I endeavoured to explain the chief points of them in a book of Meditations, which is not in itself large, but the size of which has been increased, and the matter greatly illustrated, by the Objections which several very learned persons sent to me on occasion of it, and by the Replies which I made to them. At length, after it appeared to me that those preceding treatises had sufficiently prepared the minds of my readers for the Principles of Philosophy, I also published it; and I have divided this work into four parts, the first of which contains the principles of human knowledge, and which may be called the First Philosophy, or Metaphysics. That this part, accordingly, may be properly understood, it will be necessary to read beforehand the book of Meditations I wrote on the same subject. The other three parts contain all that is most general in Physics, namely, the explication of the first laws or principles of nature, and the way in which the heavens, the fixed stars, the planets, comets, and generally the whole universe, were composed; in the next place, the explication, in particular, of the nature of this earth, the air, water, fire, the magnet, which are the bodies we most commonly find everywhere around it, and of all the qualities we observe in these bodies, as light, heat, gravity, and the like. In this way, it seems to me, I have commenced the orderly explanation of the whole of philosophy, without omitting any of the matters that ought to precede the last which I discussed. But to bring this undertaking to its conclusion, I ought hereafter to explain, in the same manner, the nature of the other more particular bodies that are on the earth, namely, minerals, plants, animals, and especially man; finally, to treat thereafter with accuracy of Medicine, Ethics, and Mechanics. I should require to do this in order to give to the world a complete body of philosophy; and I do not yet feel myself so old,- -I do not so much distrust my strength, nor do I find myself so far removed from the knowledge of what remains, as that I should not dare to undertake to complete this design, provided I were in a position to make all the experiments which I should require for the basis and verification of my reasonings. But seeing that would demand a great expenditure, to which the resources of a private individual like myself would not be adequate, unless aided by the public, and as I have no ground to expect this aid, I believe that I ought for the future to content myself with studying for my own instruction, and posterity will excuse me if I fail hereafter to labour for them.

Meanwhile, that it may be seen wherein I think I have already promoted the general good, I will here mention the fruits that may be gathered from my Principles. The first is the satisfaction which the mind will experience on finding in the work many truths before unknown; for although frequently truth does not so greatly affect our imagination as falsity and fiction, because it seems less wonderful and is more simple, yet the gratification it affords is always more durable and solid. The second fruit is, that in studying these principles we will become accustomed by degrees to judge better of all the things we come in contact with, and thus be made wiser, in which respect the effect will be quite the opposite of the common philosophy, for we may easily remark in those we call pedants that it renders them less capable of rightly exercising their reason than they would have been if they had never known it. The third is, that the truths which they contain, being highly clear and certain, will take away all ground of dispute, and thus dispose men's minds to gentleness and concord; whereas the contrary is the effect of the controversies of the schools, which, as they insensibly render those who are exercised in them more wrangling and opinionative, are perhaps the prime cause of the heresies and dissensions that now harass the world. The last and chief fruit of these Principles is, that one will be able, by cultivating them, to discover many truths I myself have not unfolded, and thus passing by degrees from one to another, to acquire in course of time a perfect knowledge of the whole of philosophy, and to rise to the highest degree of wisdom. For just as all the arts, though in their beginnings they are rude and imperfect, are yet gradually perfected by practice, from their containing at first something true, and whose effect experience evinces; so in philosophy, when we have true principles, we cannot fail by following them to meet sometimes with other truths; and we could not better prove the falsity of those of Aristotle, than by saying that men made no progress in knowledge by their means during the many ages they prosecuted them.

 I well know that there are some men so precipitate and accustomed to use so little circumspection in what they do, that, even with the most solid foundations, they could not rear a firm superstructure; and as it is usually those who are the readiest to make books, they would in a short time mar all that I have done, and introduce uncertainty and doubt into my manner of philosophizing, from which I have carefully endeavoured to banish them, if people were to receive their writings as mine, or as representing my opinions. I had, not long ago, some experience of this in one of those who were believed desirous of following me the most closely, [Footnote: Regius; see La Vie de M. Descartes, reduite en abrege (Baillet). Liv. vii., chap. vii.—T.] and one too of whom I had somewhere said that I had such confidence in his genius as to believe that he adhered to no opinions which I should not be ready to avow as mine; for he last year published a book entitled "Fundamental Physics," in which, although he seems to have written nothing on the subject of Physics and Medicine which he did not take from my writings, as well from those I have published as from another still imperfect on the nature of animals, which fell into his hands; nevertheless, because he has copied them badly, and changed the order, and denied certain metaphysical truths upon which all Physics ought to be based, I am obliged wholly to disavow his work, and here to request readers not to attribute to me any opinion unless they find it expressly stated in my own writings, and to receive no opinion as true, whether in my writings or elsewhere, unless they see that it is very clearly deduced from true principles. I well know, likewise, that many ages may elapse ere all the truths deducible from these principles are evolved out of them, as well because the greater number of such as remain to be discovered depend on certain particular experiments that never occur by chance, but which require to be investigated with care and expense by men of the highest intelligence, as because it will hardly happen that the same persons who have the sagacity to make a right use of them, will possess also the means of making them, and also because the majority of the best minds have formed so low an estimate of philosophy in general, from the imperfections they have remarked in the kind in vogue up to the present time, that they cannot apply themselves to the search after truth.

But, in conclusion, if the difference discernible between the principles in question and those of every other system, and the great array of truths deducible from them, lead them to discern the importance of continuing the search after these truths, and to observe the degree of wisdom, the perfection and felicity of life, to which they are fitted to conduct us, I venture to believe that there will not be found one who is not ready to labour hard in so profitable a study, or at least to favour and aid with all his might those who shall devote themselves to it with success.

The height of my wishes is, that posterity may sometime behold the happy issue of it, etc.

TO THE MOST SERENE PRINCESS,

ELIZABETH, ELDEST DAUGHTER OF FREDERICK, KING OF BOHEMIA, COUNT PALATINE, AND ELECTOR OF THE SACRED ROMAN EMPIRE.

MADAM,—The greatest advantage I have derived from the writings which I have already published, has arisen from my having, through means of them, become known to your Highness, and thus been privileged to hold occasional converse with one in whom so many rare and estimable qualities are united, as to lead me to believe I should do service to the public by proposing them as an example to posterity. It would ill become me to flatter, or to give expression to anything of which I had no certain knowledge, especially in the first pages of a work in which I aim at laying down the principles of truth. And the generous modesty that is conspicuous in all your actions, assures me that the frank and simple judgment of a man who only writes what he believes will be more agreeable to you than the ornate laudations of those who have studied the art of compliment. For this reason, I will give insertion to nothing in this letter for which I have not the certainty both of experience and reason; and in the exordium, as in the rest of the work, I will write only as becomes a philosopher. There is a vast difference between real and apparent virtues; and there is also a great discrepancy between those real virtues that proceed from an accurate knowledge of the truth, and such as are accompanied with ignorance or error. The virtues I call apparent are only, properly speaking, vices, which, as they are less frequent than the vices that are opposed to them, and are farther removed from them than the intermediate virtues, are usually held in higher esteem than those virtues. Thus, because those who fear dangers too much are more numerous than they who fear them too little, temerity is frequently opposed to the vice of timidity, and taken for a virtue, and is commonly more highly esteemed than true fortitude. Thus, also, the prodigal are in ordinary more praised than the liberal; and none more easily acquire a great reputation for piety than the superstitious and hypocritical. With regard to true virtues, these do not all proceed from true knowledge, for there are some that likewise spring from defect or error; thus, simplicity is frequently the source of goodness, fear of devotion, and despair of courage. The virtues that are thus accompanied with some imperfections differ from each other, and have received diverse appellations. But those pure and perfect virtues that arise from the knowledge of good alone are all of the same nature, and may be comprised under the single term wisdom. For, whoever owns the firm and constant resolution of always using his reason as well as lies in his power, and in all his actions of doing what he judges to be best, is truly wise, as far as his nature permits; and by this alone he is just, courageous, temperate, and possesses all the other virtues, but so well balanced as that none of them appears more prominent than another: and for this reason, although they are much more perfect than the virtues that blaze forth through the mixture of some defect, yet, because the crowd thus observes them less, they are not usually extolled so highly. Besides, of the two things that are requisite for the wisdom thus described, namely, the perception of the understanding and the disposition of the will, it is only that which lies in the will which all men can possess equally, inasmuch as the understanding of some is inferior to that of others. But although those who have only an inferior understanding may be as perfectly wise as their nature permits, and may render themselves highly acceptable to God by their virtue, provided they preserve always a firm and constant resolution to do all that they shall judge to be right, and to omit nothing that may lead them to the knowledge of the duties of which they are ignorant; nevertheless, those who preserve a constant resolution of performing the right, and are especially careful in instructing themselves, and who possess also a highly perspicacious intellect, arrive doubtless at a higher degree of wisdom than others; and I see that these three particulars are found in great perfection in your Highness. For, in the first place, your desire of self-instruction is manifest, from the circumstance that neither the amusements of the court, nor the accustomed mode of educating ladies, which ordinarily condemns them to ignorance, have been sufficient to prevent you from studying with much care all that is best in the arts and sciences; and the incomparable perspicacity of your intellect is evinced by this, that you penetrated the secrets of the sciences and acquired an accurate knowledge of them in a very short period. But of the vigour of your intellect I have a still stronger proof, and one peculiar to myself, in that I have never yet met any one who understood so generally and so well as yourself all that is contained in my writings. For there are several, even among men of the highest intellect and learning, who find them very obscure. And I remark, in almost all those who are versant in Metaphysics, that they are wholly disinclined from Geometry; and, on the other hand, that the cultivators of Geometry have no ability for the investigations of the First Philosophy: insomuch that I can say with truth I know but one mind, and that is your own, to which both studies are alike congenial, and which I therefore, with propriety, designate incomparable. But what most of all enhances my admiration is, that so accurate and varied an acquaintance with the whole circle of the sciences is not found in some aged doctor who has employed many years in contemplation, but in a Princess still young, and whose countenance and years would more fitly represent one of the Graces than a Muse or the sage Minerva. In conclusion, I not only remark in your Highness all that is requisite on the part of the mind to perfect and sublime wisdom, but also all that can be required on the part of the will or the manners, in which benignity and gentleness are so conjoined with majesty that, though fortune has attacked you with continued injustice, it has failed either to irritate or crush you. And this constrains me to such veneration that I not only think this work due to you, since it treats of philosophy which is the study of wisdom, but likewise feel not more zeal for my reputation as a philosopher than pleasure in subscribing myself,—

Of your most Serene Highness, The most devoted servant,
DESCARTES.

OF THE PRINCIPLES OF HUMAN KNOWLEDGE.

I. THAT in order to seek truth, it is necessary once in the course of our life, to doubt, as far as possible, of all things.

As we were at one time children, and as we formed various judgments regarding the objects presented to our senses, when as yet we had not the entire use of our reason, numerous prejudices stand in the way of our arriving at the knowledge of truth; and of these it seems impossible for us to rid ourselves, unless we undertake, once in our lifetime, to doubt of all those things in which we may discover even the smallest suspicion of uncertainty.

II. That we ought also to consider as false all that is doubtful.

Moreover, it will be useful likewise to esteem as false the things of which we shall be able to doubt, that we may with greater clearness discover what possesses most certainty and is the easiest to know.

III. That we ought not meanwhile to make use of doubt in the conduct of life.

In the meantime, it is to be observed that we are to avail ourselves of this general doubt only while engaged in the contemplation of truth. For, as far as concerns the conduct of life, we are very frequently obliged to follow opinions merely probable, or even sometimes, though of two courses of action we may not perceive more probability in the one than in the other, to choose one or other, seeing the opportunity of acting would not unfrequently pass away before we could free ourselves from our doubts.

IV. Why we may doubt of sensible things.

Accordingly, since we now only design to apply ourselves to the investigation of truth, we will doubt, first, whether of all the things that have ever fallen under our senses, or which we have ever imagined, any one really exist; in the first place, because we know by experience that the senses sometimes err, and it would be imprudent to trust too much to what has even once deceived us; secondly, because in dreams we perpetually seem to perceive or imagine innumerable objects which have no existence. And to one who has thus resolved upon a general doubt, there appear no marks by which he can with certainty distinguish sleep from the waking state.

V. Why we may also doubt of mathematical demonstrations.

We will also doubt of the other things we have before held as most certain, even of the demonstrations of mathematics, and of their principles which we have hitherto deemed self-evident; in the first place, because we have sometimes seen men fall into error in such matters, and admit as absolutely certain and self evident what to us appeared false, but chiefly because we have learnt that God who created us is all-powerful; for we do not yet know whether perhaps it was his will to create us so that we are always deceived, even in the things we think we know best: since this does not appear more impossible than our being occasionally deceived, which, however, as observation teaches us, is the case. And if we suppose that an all- powerful God is not the author of our being, and that we exist of ourselves or by some other means, still, the less powerful we suppose our author to be, the greater reason will we have for believing that we are not so perfect as that we may not be continually deceived.

VI. That we possess a free-will, by which we can withhold our assent from what is doubtful, and thus avoid error.

But meanwhile, whoever in the end may be the author of our being, and however powerful and deceitful he may be, we are nevertheless conscious of a freedom, by which we can refrain from admitting to a place in our belief aught that is not manifestly certain and undoubted, and thus guard against ever being deceived.

VII. That we cannot doubt of our existence while we doubt, and that this is the first knowledge we acquire when we philosophize in order.

While we thus reject all of which we can entertain the smallest doubt, and even imagine that it is false, we easily indeed suppose that there is neither God, nor sky, nor bodies, and that we ourselves even have neither hands nor feet, nor, finally, a body;

but we cannot in the same way suppose that we are not while we doubt of the truth of these things; for there is a repugnance in conceiving that what thinks does not exist at the very time when it thinks. Accordingly, the knowledge, *I* THINK, THEREFORE *I* AM, is the first and most certain that occurs to one who philosophizes orderly.

VIII. That we hence discover the distinction between the mind and the body, or between a thinking and corporeal thing.

And this is the best mode of discovering the nature of the mind, and its distinctness from the body: for examining what we are, while supposing, as we now do, that there is nothing really existing apart from our thought, we clearly perceive that neither extension, nor figure, nor local motion,[Footnote: Instead of "local motion," the French has "existence in any place."] nor anything similar that can be attributed to body, pertains to our nature, and nothing save thought alone; and, consequently, that the notion we have of our mind precedes that of any corporeal thing, and is more certain, seeing we still doubt whether there is any body in existence, while we already perceive that we think.

IX. What thought (COGITATIO) is.

By the word thought, I understand all that which so takes place in us that we of ourselves are immediately conscious of it; and, accordingly, not only to understand (INTELLIGERE, ENTENDRE), to will (VELLE), to imagine (IMAGINARI), but even to perceive (SENTIRE, SENTIR), are here the same as to think (COGITARE, PENSER). For if I say, I see, or, I walk, therefore I am; and if I understand by vision or walking the act of my eyes or of my limbs, which is the work of the body, the conclusion is not absolutely certain, because, as is often the case in dreams, I may think that I see or walk, although I do not open my eyes or move from my place, and even, perhaps, although I have no body: but, if I mean the sensation itself, or consciousness of seeing or walking, the knowledge is manifestly certain, because it is then referred to the mind, which alone perceives or is conscious that it sees or walks. [Footnote: In the French, "which alone has the power of perceiving, or of being conscious in any other way whatever."]

X. That the notions which are simplest and self-evident, are obscured by logical definitions; and that such are not to be reckoned among the cognitions acquired by study, [but as born with us].

I do not here explain several other terms which I have used, or design to use in the sequel, because their meaning seems to me sufficiently self-evident. And I frequently remarked that philosophers erred in attempting to explain, by logical definitions, such truths as are most simple and self-evident; for they thus only rendered them more obscure. And when I said that the proposition, *I* THINK, THEREFORE *I* AM, is of all others the first and most certain which occurs to one philosophizing orderly, I did not therefore deny that it was necessary to know what thought, existence, and certitude are, and the truth that, in order to think it is necessary to be, and the like; but, because these are the most simple notions, and such as of themselves afford the knowledge of nothing existing, I did not judge it proper there to enumerate them.

XI. How we can know our mind more clearly than our body.

But now that it may be discerned how the knowledge we have of the mind not only precedes, and has greater certainty, but is even clearer, than that we have of the body, it must be remarked, as a matter that is highly manifest by the natural light, that to nothing no affections or qualities belong; and, accordingly, that where we observe certain affections, there a thing or substance to which these pertain, is necessarily found. The same light also shows us that we know a thing or substance more clearly in proportion as we discover in it a greater number of qualities. Now, it is manifest that we remark a greater number of qualities in our mind than in any other thing; for there is no occasion on which we know anything whatever when we are not at the same time led with much greater certainty to the knowledge of our own mind. For example, if I judge that there is an earth because I touch or see it, on the same ground, and with still greater reason, I must be persuaded that my mind exists; for it may be, perhaps, that I think I touch the earth while there is one in existence; but it is not possible that I should so judge, and my mind which thus judges not exist; and the same holds good of whatever object is presented to our mind.

XII. How it happens that every one does not come equally to know this.

Those who have not philosophized in order have had other opinions on this subject, because they never distinguished with sufficient care the mind from the body. For, although they had no difficulty in believing that they themselves existed, and that they had a higher assurance of this than of any other thing, nevertheless, as they did not observe that by THEMSELVES, they ought here to understand their MINDS alone [when the question related to metaphysical certainty]; and since, on the contrary, they rather meant their bodies which they saw with their eyes, touched with their hands, and to which they erroneously attributed the faculty of perception, they were prevented from distinctly apprehending the nature of the mind.

XIII. In what sense the knowledge of other things depends upon the knowledge of God.

But when the mind, which thus knows itself but is still in doubt as to all other things, looks around on all sides, with a view to the farther extension of its knowledge, it first of all discovers within itself the ideas of many things; and while it simply contemplates them, and neither affirms nor denies that there is anything beyond itself corresponding to them, it is in no danger of erring. The mind also discovers certain common notions out of which it frames various demonstrations that carry conviction to such a degree as to render doubt of their truth impossible, so long as we give attention to them. For example, the mind has within itself ideas of numbers and figures, and it has likewise among its common notions the principle THAT IF EQUALS BE ADDED TO EQUALS THE WHOLES WILL BE EQUAL and the like; from which it is easy to demonstrate that the three angles of a triangle are equal to two right angles, etc. Now, so long as we attend to the premises from which this conclusion and others similar to it were deduced, we feel assured of their truth; but, as the mind cannot always think of these with attention, when it has the remembrance of a conclusion without recollecting the order of its deduction, and is uncertain whether the author of its being has created it of a nature that is liable to be deceived, even in what appears most evident, it perceives that there is just ground to distrust the truth of such conclusions, and that it cannot possess any certain knowledge until it has discovered its author.

XIV. That we may validly infer the existence of God from necessary existence being comprised in the concept we have of him.

When the mind afterwards reviews the different ideas that are in it, it discovers what is by far the chief among them—that of a Being omniscient, all-powerful, and absolutely perfect; and it observes that in this idea there is contained not only possible and contingent existence, as in the ideas of all other things which it clearly perceives, but existence absolutely necessary and eternal. And just as because, for example, the equality of its three angles to two right angles is necessarily comprised in the idea of a triangle, the mind is firmly persuaded that the three angles of a triangle are equal to two right angles; so, from its perceiving necessary and eternal existence to be comprised in the idea which it has of an all-perfect Being, it ought manifestly to conclude that this all-perfect Being exists.

XV. That necessary existence is not in the same way comprised in the notions which we have of other things, but merely contingent existence.

The mind will be still more certain of the truth of this conclusion, if it consider that it has no idea of any other thing in which it can discover that necessary existence is contained; for, from this circumstance alone, it will discern that the idea of an all-perfect Being has not been framed by itself, and that it does not represent a chimera, but a true and immutable nature, which must exist since it can only be conceived as necessarily existing.

XVI. That prejudices hinder many from clearly knowing the necessity of the existence of God.

Our mind would have no difficulty in assenting to this truth, if it were, first of all, wholly free from prejudices; but as we have been accustomed to distinguish, in all other things, essence from existence, and to imagine at will many ideas of things which neither are nor have been, it easily happens, when we do not steadily fix our thoughts on the contemplation of the all-perfect Being, that a doubt arises as to whether the idea we have of him is not one of those which we frame at pleasure, or at least of that class to whose essence existence does not pertain.

XVII. That the greater objective (representative) perfection there is in our idea of a thing, the greater also must be the perfection of its cause.

When we further reflect on the various ideas that are in us, it is easy to perceive that there is not much difference among them, when we consider them simply as certain modes of thinking, but that they are widely different, considered in reference to the objects they represent; and that their causes must be so much the more perfect according to the degree of objective perfection contained in them. [Footnote: "as what they represent of their object has more perfection."—FRENCH.] For there is no difference between this and the case of a person who has the idea of a machine, in the construction of which great skill is displayed, in which circumstances we have a right to inquire how he came by this idea, whether, for example, he somewhere saw such a machine constructed by another, or whether he was so accurately taught the mechanical sciences, or is endowed with such force of genius, that he was able of himself to invent it, without having elsewhere seen anything like it; for all the ingenuity which is contained in the idea objectively only, or as it were in a picture, must exist at least in its first and chief cause, whatever that may be, not only objectively or representatively, but in truth formally or eminently.

XVIII. That the existence of God may be again inferred from the above.

Thus, because we discover in our minds the idea of God, or of an all-perfect Being, we have a right to inquire into the source whence we derive it; and we will discover that the perfections it represents are so immense as to render it quite certain that we could only derive it from an all-perfect Being; that is, from a God really existing. For it is not only manifest by the natural light that nothing cannot be the cause of anything whatever, and that the more perfect cannot arise from the less perfect, so as to be thereby produced as by its efficient and total cause, but also that it is impossible we can have the idea or representation of anything whatever, unless there be somewhere, either in us or out of us, an original which comprises, in reality, all the perfections that are thus represented to us; but, as we do not in any way find in ourselves those absolute perfections of which we have the idea, we must conclude that they exist in some nature different from ours, that is, in God, or at least that they were once in him; and it most manifestly follows [from their infinity] that they are still there.

XIX. That, although we may not comprehend the nature of God, there is yet nothing which we know so clearly as his perfections.

This will appear sufficiently certain and manifest to those who have been accustomed to contemplate the idea of God, and to turn their thoughts to his infinite perfections; for, although we may not comprehend them, because it is of the nature of the infinite not to be comprehended by what is finite, we nevertheless conceive them more clearly and distinctly than material objects, for this reason, that, being simple, and unobscured by limits,[Footnote: After LIMITS, "what of them we do conceive is much less confused. There is, besides, no speculation more calculated to aid in perfecting our understanding, and which is more important than this, inasmuch as the consideration of an object that has no limits to its perfections fills us with satisfaction and assurance."-FRENCH.] they occupy our mind more fully.

XX. That we are not the cause of ourselves, but that this is God,

and consequently that there is a God.

But, because every one has not observed this, and because, when we have an idea of any machine in which great skill is displayed, we usually know with sufficient accuracy the manner in which we obtained it, and as we cannot even recollect when the idea we have of a God was communicated to us by him, seeing it was always in our minds, it is still necessary that we should continue our review, and make inquiry after our author, possessing, as we do, the idea of the infinite perfections of a God: for it is in the highest degree evident by the natural light, that that which knows something more perfect than itself, is not the source of its own being, since it would thus have given to itself all the perfections which it knows; and that, consequently, it could draw its origin from no other being than from him who possesses in himself all those perfections, that is, from God.

XXI. That the duration alone of our life is sufficient to demonstrate the existence of God.

The truth of this demonstration will clearly appear, provided we consider the nature of time, or the duration of things; for this is of such a kind that its parts are not mutually dependent, and never co-existent; and, accordingly, from the fact that we now are, it does not necessarily follow that we shall be a moment afterwards, unless some cause, viz., that which first produced us, shall, as it were, continually reproduce us, that is, conserve us. For we easily understand that there is no power in us by which we can conserve ourselves, and that the being who has so much power as to conserve us out of himself, must also by so much the greater reason conserve himself, or rather stand in need of being conserved by no one whatever, and, in fine, be God.

XXII. That in knowing the existence of God, in the manner here explained, we likewise know all his attributes, as far as they can be known by the natural light alone.

There is the great advantage in proving the existence of God in this way, viz., by his idea, that we at the same time know what he is, as far as the weakness of our nature allows; for, reflecting on the idea we have of him which is born with us, we perceive that he is eternal, omniscient, omnipotent, the source of all goodness and truth, creator of all things, and that, in fine, he has in himself all that in which we can clearly discover any infinite perfection or good that is not limited by any imperfection.

XXIII. That God is not corporeal, and does not perceive by means of senses as we do, or will the evil of sin.

For there are indeed many things in the world that are to a certain extent imperfect or limited, though possessing also some perfection; and it is accordingly impossible that any such can be in God. Thus, looking to corporeal nature,[Footnote: In the French, "since extension constitutes the nature of body."] since divisibility is included in local extension, and this indicates imperfection, it is certain that God is not body. And although in men it is to some degree a perfection to be capable of perceiving by means of the senses, nevertheless since in every sense there is passivity [Footnote: In the French, "because our perceptions arise from impressions made upon us from another source," i.e., than ourselves.] which indicates dependency, we must conclude that God is in no manner possessed of senses, and that he only understands and wills, not, however, like us, by acts in any way distinct, but always by an act that is one, identical, and the simplest possible, understands, wills, and operates all, that is, all things that in reality exist; for he does not will the evil of sin, seeing this is but the negation of being.

XXIV. That in passing from the knowledge of God to the knowledge of the creatures, it is necessary to remember that our understanding is finite, and the power of God infinite.

But as we know that God alone is the true cause of all that is or can be, we will doubtless follow the best way of philosophizing, if, from the knowledge we have of God himself, we pass to the explication of the things which he has created, and essay to deduce it from the notions that are naturally in our minds, for we will thus obtain the most perfect science, that is, the knowledge of effects through their causes. But that we may be able to make this attempt with sufficient security from error, we must use the precaution to bear in mind as much as possible that

God, who is the author of things, is infinite, while we are wholly finite.

XXV. That we must believe all that God has revealed, although it may surpass the reach of our faculties.

Thus, if perhaps God reveal to us or others, matters concerning himself which surpass the natural powers of our mind, such as the mysteries of the incarnation and of the trinity, we will not refuse to believe them, although we may not clearly understand them; nor will we be in any way surprised to find in the immensity of his nature, or even in what he has created, many things that exceed our comprehension.

XXVI. That it is not needful to enter into disputes [Footnote: "to essay to comprehend the infinite."—FRENCH.] regarding the infinite, but merely to hold all that in which we can find no limits as indefinite, such as the extension of the world, the divisibility of the parts of matter, the number of the stars, etc.

We will thus never embarrass ourselves by disputes about the infinite, seeing it would be absurd for us who are finite to undertake to determine anything regarding it, and thus as it were to limit it by endeavouring to comprehend it. We will accordingly give ourselves no concern to reply to those who demand whether the half of an infinite line is also infinite, and whether an infinite number is even or odd, and the like, because it is only such as imagine their minds to be infinite who seem bound to entertain questions of this sort. And, for our part, looking to all those things in which in certain senses, we discover no limits, we will not, therefore, affirm that they are infinite, but will regard them simply as indefinite. Thus, because we cannot imagine extension so great that we cannot still conceive greater, we will say that the magnitude of possible things is indefinite, and because a body cannot be divided into parts so small that each of these may not be conceived as again divided into others still smaller, let us regard quantity as divisible into parts whose number is indefinite; and as we cannot imagine so many stars that it would seem impossible for God to create more, let us suppose that their number is indefinite, and so in other instances.

XXVII. What difference there is between the indefinite and the infinite.

And we will call those things indefinite rather than infinite, with the view of reserving to God alone the appellation of infinite; in the first place, because not only do we discover in him alone no limits on any side, but also because we positively conceive that he admits of none; and in the second place, because we do not in the same way positively conceive that other things are in every part unlimited, but merely negatively admit that their limits, if they have any, cannot be discovered by us.

XXVIII. That we must examine, not the final, but the efficient, causes of created things.

Likewise, finally, we will not seek reasons of natural things from the end which God or nature proposed to himself in their creation (i. e., final causes), [Footnote: "We will not stop to consider the ends which God proposed to himself in the creation of the world, and we will entirely reject from our philosophy the search of final causes!"—French.] for we ought not to presume so far as to think that we are sharers in the counsels of Deity, but, considering him as the efficient cause of all things, let us endeavour to discover by the natural light [Footnote: "Faculty of reasoning."—FRENCH.] which he has planted in us, applied to those of his attributes of which he has been willing we should have some knowledge, what must be concluded regarding those effects we perceive by our senses; bearing in mind, however, what has been already said, that we must only confide in this natural light so long as nothing contrary to its dictates is revealed by God himself. [Footnote: The last clause, beginning "bearing in mind." is omitted in the French.]

XXIX. That God is not the cause of our errors.

The first attribute of God which here falls to be considered, is that he is absolutely veracious and the source of all light, so that it is plainly repugnant for him to deceive us, or to be properly and positively the cause of the errors to which we are consciously subject; for although the address to deceive seems to be some mark of subtlety of mind among men, yet without doubt the will to deceive only proceeds from malice or from fear and weakness, and consequently cannot be attributed to God.

XXX. That consequently all which we clearly perceive is true, and that we are thus delivered from the doubts above proposed.

Whence it follows, that the light of nature, or faculty of knowledge given us by God, can never compass any object which is not true, in as far as it attains to a knowledge of it, that is, in as far as the object is clearly and distinctly apprehended. For God would have merited the appellation of a deceiver if he had given us this faculty perverted, and such as might lead us to take falsity for truth [when we used it aright]. Thus the highest doubt is removed, which arose from our ignorance on the point as to whether perhaps our nature was such that we might be deceived even in those things that appear to us the most evident. The same principle ought also to be of avail against all the other grounds of doubting that have been already enumerated. For mathematical truths ought now to be above suspicion, since these are of the clearest. And if we perceive anything by our senses, whether while awake or asleep, we will easily discover the truth provided we separate what there is of clear and distinct in the knowledge from what is obscure and confused. There is no need that I should here say more on this subject, since it has already received ample treatment in the metaphysical Meditations; and what follows will serve to explain it still more accurately.

XXXI. That our errors are, in respect of God, merely negations, but, in respect of ourselves, privations.

But as it happens that we frequently fall into error, although God is no deceiver, if we desire to inquire into the origin and cause of our errors, with a view to guard against them, it is necessary to observe that they depend less on our understanding than on our will, and that they have no need of the actual concourse of God, in order to their production; so that, when considered in reference to God, they are merely negations, but in reference to ourselves, privations.

XXXII. That there are only two modes of thinking in us, viz., the perception of the understanding and the action of the will.

For all the modes of thinking of which we are conscious may be referred to two general classes, the one of which is the perception or operation of the understanding, and the other the volition or operation of the will. Thus, to perceive by the senses (SENTIRE), to imagine, and to conceive things purely intelligible, are only different modes of perceiving (PERCIPIENDI); but to desire, to be averse from, to affirm, to deny, to doubt, are different modes of willing.

XXXIII. That we never err unless when we judge of something which we do not sufficiently apprehend.

When we apprehend anything we are in no danger of error, if we refrain from judging of it in any way; and even when we have formed a judgment regarding it, we would never fall into error, provided we gave our assent only to what we clearly and distinctly perceived; but the reason why we are usually deceived, is that we judge without possessing an exact knowledge of that of which we judge.

XXXIV. That the will as well as the understanding is required for judging.

I admit that the understanding is necessary for judging, there being no room to suppose that we can judge of that which we in no way apprehend; but the will also is required in order to our assenting to what we have in any degree perceived. It is not necessary, however, at least to form any judgment whatever, that we have an entire and perfect apprehension of a thing; for we may assent to many things of which we have only a very obscure and confused knowledge.

XXXV. That the will is of greater extension than the understanding, and is thus the source of our errors.

Further, the perception of the intellect extends only to the few things that are presented to it, and is always very limited: the will, on the other hand, may, in a certain sense, be said to be infinite, because we observe nothing that can be the object of the will of any other, even of the unlimited will of God, to which ours cannot also extend, so that we easily carry it beyond the objects we clearly perceive; and when we do this, it is not wonderful that we happen to be deceived.

XXXVI. That our errors cannot be imputed to God.

But although God has not given us an omniscient understanding, he is not on this account to be considered in any wise the author of our errors, for it is of the nature of created intellect to be finite, and of finite intellect not to embrace all things.

XXXVII. That the chief perfection of man is his being able to act freely or by will, and that it is this which renders him worthy of praise or blame.

That the will should be the more extensive is in harmony with its nature: and it is a high perfection in man to be able to act by means of it, that is, freely; and thus in a peculiar way to be the master of his own actions, and merit praise or blame. For self-acting machines are not commended because they perform with exactness all the movements for which they were adapted, seeing their motions are carried on necessarily; but the maker of them is praised on account of the exactness with which they were framed, because he did not act of necessity, but freely; and, on the same principle, we must attribute to ourselves something more on this account, that when we embrace truth, we do so not of necessity, but freely.

XXXVIII. That error is a defect in our mode of acting, not in our nature; and that the faults of their subjects may be frequently attributed to other masters, but never to God.

It is true, that as often as we err, there is some defect in our mode of action or in the use of our liberty, but not in our nature, because this is always the same, whether our judgments be true or false. And although God could have given to us such perspicacity of intellect that we should never have erred, we have, notwithstanding, no right to demand this of him; for, although with us he who was able to prevent evil and did not is held guilty of it, God is not in the same way to be reckoned responsible for our errors because he had the power to prevent them, inasmuch as the dominion which some men possess over others has been instituted for the purpose of enabling them to hinder those under them from doing evil, whereas the dominion which God exercises over the universe is perfectly absolute and free. For this reason we ought to thank him for the goods he has given us, and not complain that he has not blessed us with all which we know it was in his power to impart.

XXXIX. That the liberty of our will is self-evident.

Finally, it is so manifest that we possess a free will, capable of giving or withholding its assent, that this truth must be reckoned among the first and most common notions which are born with us. This, indeed, has already very clearly appeared, for when essaying to doubt of all things, we went so far as to suppose even that he who created us employed his limitless power in deceiving us in every way, we were conscious nevertheless of being free to abstain from believing what was not in every respect certain and undoubted. Bat that of which we are unable to doubt at such a time is as self- evident and clear as any thing we can ever know.

XL. That it is likewise certain that God has fore-ordained all things.

But because what we have already discovered of God, gives us the assurance that his power is so immense that we would sin in thinking ourselves capable of ever doing anything which he had not ordained beforehand, we should soon be embarrassed in great difficulties if we undertook to harmonise the pre-ordination of God with the freedom of our will, and endeavoured to comprehend both truths at once.

XLI. How the freedom of our will may be reconciled with the Divine pre-ordination.

But, in place of this, we will be free from these embarrassments if we recollect that our mind is limited, while the power of God, by which he not only knew from all eternity what is or can be, but also willed and pre-ordained it, is infinite. It thus happens that we possess sufficient intelligence to know clearly and distinctly that this power is in God, but not enough to comprehend how he leaves the free actions of men indeterminate} and, on the other hand, we have such consciousness of the liberty and indifference which exists in ourselves, that there is nothing we more clearly or perfectly comprehend: [so that the omnipotence of God ought not to keep us from believing it]. For it would be absurd to doubt of that of which we are fully conscious, and which we experience as existing in ourselves, because we do not comprehend another matter which, from its very nature, we know to be incomprehensible.

XLII. *How, although we never will to err, it is nevertheless by our will that we do err.*

But now since we know that all our errors depend upon our will, and as no one wishes to deceive himself, it may seem wonderful that there is any error in our judgments at all. It is necessary to remark, however, that there is a great difference between willing to be deceived, and willing to yield assent to opinions in which it happens that error is found. For though there is no one who expressly wishes to fall into error, we will yet hardly find any one who is not ready to assent to things in which, unknown to himself, error lurks; and it even frequently happens that it is the desire itself of following after truth that leads those not fully aware of the order in which it ought to be sought for, to pass judgment on matters of which they have no adequate knowledge, and thus to fall into error.

XLIII. *That we shall never err if we give our assent only to what we clearly and distinctly perceive.*

But it is certain we will never admit falsity for truth, so long as we judge only of that which we clearly and distinctly perceive; because, as God is no deceiver, the faculty of knowledge which he has given us cannot be fallacious, nor, for the same reason, the faculty of will, when we do not extend it beyond the objects we clearly know. And even although this truth could not be established by reasoning, the minds of all have been so impressed by nature as spontaneously to assent to whatever is clearly perceived, and to experience an impossibility to doubt of its truth.

XLIV. That we uniformly judge improperly when we assent to what we do not clearly perceive, although our judgment may chance to be true; and that it is frequently our memory which deceives us by leading us to believe that certain things were formerly sufficiently understood by us.

It is likewise certain that, when we approve of any reason which we do not apprehend, we are either deceived, or, if we stumble on the truth, it is only by chance, and thus we can never possess the assurance that we are not in error. I confess it seldom happens that we judge of a thing when we have observed we do not apprehend it, because it is a dictate of the natural light never to judge of what we do not know. But we most frequently err in this, that we presume upon a past knowledge of much to which we give our assent, as to something treasured up in the memory, and perfectly known to us; whereas, in truth, we have no such knowledge.

XLV. What constitutes clear and distinct perception.

There are indeed a great many persons who, through their whole lifetime, never perceive anything in a way necessary for judging of it properly; for the knowledge upon which we can establish a certain and indubitable judgment must be not only clear, but also, distinct. I call that clear which is present and manifest to the mind giving attention to it, just as we are said clearly to see objects when, being present to the eye looking on, they stimulate it with sufficient force. and it is disposed to regard them; but the distinct is that which is so precise and different from all other objects as to comprehend in itself only what is clear. [Footnote: "what appears manifestly to him who considers it as he ought."— FRENCH.]

XLVI. It is shown, from the example of pain, that a perception may be clear without being distinct, but that it cannot be distinct unless it is clear.

For example, when any one feels intense pain, the knowledge which he has of this pain is very clear, but it is not always distinct; for men usually confound it with the obscure judgment they form regarding its nature, and think that there is in the suffering part something similar to the sensation of pain of which they are alone conscious. And thus perception may be clear without being distinct, but it can never be distinct without likewise being clear.

XLVII. That, to correct the prejudices of our early years, we must consider what is clear in each of our simple [Footnote: "first."— FRENCH.] notions.

And, indeed, in our early years, the mind was so immersed in the body, that, although it perceived many things with sufficient clearness, it yet knew nothing distinctly; and since even at that time we exercised our judgment in many matters, numerous prejudices were thus contracted, which, by the majority, are never afterwards laid aside. But that we may now be in a position to get rid of these, I will here briefly enumerate all the simple notions of which our thoughts are composed, and distinguish in each what is clear from what is obscure, or fitted to lead into error.

XLVIII. That all the objects of our knowledge are to be regarded either (1) as things or the affections of things: or (2) as eternal truths; with the enumeration of things.

Whatever objects fall under our knowledge we consider either as things or the affections of things,[Footnote: Things and the affections of things are (in the French) equivalent to "what has some (i.e., a REAL) existence," as opposed to the class of "eternal truths," which have merely an IDEAL existence.] or as eternal truths possessing no existence beyond our thought. Of the first class the most general are substance, duration, order, number, and perhaps also some others, which notions apply to all the kinds of things. I do not, however, recognise more than two highest kinds (SUMMA GENERA) of things; the first of intellectual things, or such as have the power of thinking, including mind or thinking substance and its properties; the second, of material things, embracing extended substance, or body and its properties. Perception, volition, and all modes as well of knowing as of willing, are related to thinking substance; on the other hand, to extended substance we refer magnitude, or extension in length, breadth, and depth, figure, motion, situation, divisibility of parts themselves, and the like. There are, however, besides these, certain things of which we have an internal experience that ought not to be referred either to the mind of itself, or to the body alone, but to the close and intimate union between them, as will hereafter be shown in its place. Of this class are the appetites of hunger and thirst, etc., and also the emotions or passions of the mind which are not exclusively mental affections, as the emotions of anger, joy, sadness, love, etc.; and, finally, all the sensations, as of pain, titillation, light and colours, sounds, smells, tastes, heat, hardness, and the other tactile qualities.

XLIX. *That the eternal truths cannot be thus enumerated, but that this is not necessary.*

What I have already enumerated we are to regard as things, or the qualities or modes of things. We now come to speak of eternal truths. When we apprehend that it is impossible a thing can arise from nothing, this proposition, EX NIHILO NIHIL FIT, is not considered as somewhat existing, or as the mode of a thing, but as an eternal truth having its seat in our mind, and is called a common notion or axiom. Of this class are the following:—It is impossible the same thing can at once be and not be; what is done cannot be undone; he who thinks must exist while he thinks; and innumerable others, the whole of which it is indeed difficult to enumerate, but this is not necessary, since, if blinded by no prejudices, we cannot fail to know them when the occasion of thinking them occurs.

L. *That these truths are clearly perceived, but not equally by all men, on account of prejudices.*

And, indeed, with regard to these common notions, it is not to be doubted that they can be clearly and distinctly known, for otherwise they would not merit this appellation: as, in truth, some of them are not, with respect to all men, equally deserving of the name, because they are not equally admitted by all: not, however, from this reason, as I think, that the faculty of knowledge of one man extends farther than that of another, but rather because these common notions are opposed to the prejudices of some, who, on this account, are not able readily to embrace them, even although others, who are free from those prejudices, apprehend them with the greatest clearness.

LI. What substance is, and that the term is not applicable to God and the creatures in the same sense.

But with regard to what we consider as things or the modes of things, it is worth while to examine each of them by itself. By substance we can conceive nothing else than a thing which exists in such a way as to stand in need of nothing beyond itself in order to its existence. And, in truth, there can be conceived but one substance which is absolutely independent, and that is God. We perceive that all other things can exist only by help of the concourse of God. And, accordingly, the term substance does not apply to God and the creatures UNIVOCALLY, to adopt a term familiar in the schools; that is, no signification of this word can be distinctly understood which is common to God and them.

LII. That the term is applicable univocally to the mind and the body, and how substance itself is known.

Created substances, however, whether corporeal or thinking, may be conceived under this common concept; for these are things which, in order to their existence, stand in need of nothing but the concourse of God. But yet substance cannot be first discovered merely from its being a thing which exists independently, for existence by itself is not observed by us. We easily, however, discover substance itself from any attribute of it, by this common notion, that of nothing there are no attributes, properties, or qualities: for, from perceiving that some attribute is present, we infer that some existing thing or substance to which it may be attributed is also of necessity present.

LIII. That of every substance there is one principal attribute, as thinking of the mind, extension of the body.

But, although any attribute is sufficient to lead us to the knowledge of substance, there is, however, one principal property of every substance, which constitutes its nature or essence, and upon which all the others depend. Thus, extension in length, breadth, and depth, constitutes the nature of corporeal substance; and thought the nature of thinking substance. For every other thing that can be attributed to body, presupposes extension, and is only some mode of an extended thing; as all the properties we discover in the mind are only diverse modes of thinking. Thus, for example, we cannot conceive figure unless in something extended, nor motion unless in extended space, nor imagination, sensation, or will, unless in a thinking thing. But, on the other hand, we can conceive extension without figure or motion, and thought without imagination or sensation, and so of the others; as is clear to any one who attends to these matters.

LIV. How we may have clear and distinct notions of the substance which thinks, of that which is corporeal, and of God.

And thus we may easily have two clear and distinct notions or ideas, the one of created substance, which thinks, the other of corporeal substance, provided we carefully distinguish all the attributes of thought from those of extension. We may also have a clear and distinct idea of an uncreated and independent thinking substance, that is, of God, provided we do not suppose that this idea adequately represents to us all that is in God, and do not mix up with it anything fictitious, but attend simply to the characters that are comprised in the notion we have of him, and which we clearly know to belong to the nature of an absolutely perfect Being. For no one can deny that there is in us such an idea of God, without groundlessly supposing that there is no knowledge of God at all in the human mind.

LV. How duration, order, and number may be also distinctly conceived.

We will also have most distinct conceptions of duration, order, and number, if, in place of mixing up with our notions of them that which properly belongs to the concept of substance, we merely think that the duration of a thing is a mode under which we conceive this thing, in so far as it continues to exist; and, in like manner, that order and number are not in reality different from things disposed in order and numbered, but only modes under which we diversely consider these things.

LVI. What are modes, qualities, attributes.

And, indeed, we here understand by modes the same with what we elsewhere designate attributes or qualities. But when we consider substance as affected or varied by them, we use the term modes; when from this variation it may be denominated of such a kind, we adopt the term qualities [to designate the different modes which cause it to be so named]; and, finally, when we simply regard these modes as in the substance, we call them attributes. Accordingly, since God must be conceived as superior to change, it is not proper to say that there are modes or qualities in him, but simply attributes; and even in created things that which is found in them always in the same mode, as existence and duration in the thing which exists and endures, ought to be called attribute and not mode or quality.

LVII. That some attributes exist in the things to which they are attributed, and others only in our thought; and what duration and time are.

Of these attributes or modes there are some which exist in the things themselves, and others that have only an existence in our thought; thus, for example, time, which we distinguish from duration taken in its generality, and call the measure of motion, is only a certain mode under which we think duration itself, for we do not indeed conceive the duration of things that are moved to be different from the duration of things that are not moved: as is evident from this, that if two bodies are in motion for an hour, the one moving quickly and the other slowly, we do not reckon more time in the one than in the other, although there may be much more motion in the one of the bodies than in the other. But that we may comprehend the duration of all things under a common measure, we compare their duration with that of the greatest and most regular motions that give rise to years and days, and which we call time; hence what is so designated is nothing superadded to duration, taken in its generality, but a mode of thinking.

LVIII. That number and all universals are only modes of thought.

In the same way number, when it is not considered as in created things, but merely in the abstract or in general, is only a mode of thinking; and the same is true of all those general ideas we call universals.

LIX. How universals are formed; and what are the five common, viz., genus, species, difference, property, and accident.

Universals arise merely from our making use of one and the same idea in thinking of all individual objects between which there subsists a certain likeness; and when we comprehend all the objects represented by this idea under one name, this term likewise becomes universal. For example, when we see two stones, and do not regard their nature farther than to remark that there are two of them, we form the idea of a certain number, which we call the binary; and when we afterwards see two birds or two trees, and merely take notice of them so far as to observe that there are two of them, we again take up the same idea as before, which is, accordingly, universal; and we likewise give to this number the same universal appellation of binary. In the same way, when we consider a figure of three sides, we form a certain idea, which we call the idea of a triangle, and we afterwards make use of it as the universal to represent to our mind all other figures of three sides. But when we remark more particularly that of figures of three sides, some have a right angle and others not, we form the universal idea of a right-angled triangle, which being related to the preceding as more general, may be called species; and the right angle the universal difference by which right-angled triangles are distinguished from all others; and farther, because the square of the side which sustains the right angle is equal to the squares of the other two sides, and because this property belongs only to this species of triangles, we may call it the universal property of the species. Finally, if we suppose that of these triangles some are moved and others not, this will be their universal accident; and, accordingly, we commonly reckon five universals, viz., genus, species, difference, property, accident.

LX. Of distinctions; and first of the real.

But number in things themselves arises from the distinction there is between them: and distinction is threefold, viz., real, modal, and of reason. The real properly subsists between two or more substances; and it is sufficient to assure us that two substances are really mutually distinct, if only we are able clearly and distinctly to conceive the one of them without the other. For the knowledge we have of God renders it certain that he can effect all that of which we have a distinct idea: wherefore, since we have now, for example, the idea of an extended and corporeal substance, though we as yet do not know with certainty whether any such thing is really existent, nevertheless, merely because we have the idea of it, we may be assured that such may exist; and, if it really exists, that every part which we can determine by thought must be really distinct from the other parts of the same substance. In the same way, since every one is conscious that he thinks, and that he in thought can exclude from himself every other substance, whether thinking or extended, it is certain that each of us thus considered is really distinct from every other thinking and corporeal substance. And although we suppose that God united a body to a soul so closely that it was impossible to form a more intimate union, and thus made a composite whole, the two substances would remain really distinct, notwithstanding this union; for with whatever tie God connected them, he was not able to rid himself of the power he possessed of separating them, or of conserving the one apart from the other, and the things which God can separate or conserve separately are really distinct.

LXI. Of the modal distinction.

There are two kinds of modal distinctions, viz., that between the mode properly so-called and the substance of which it is a mode, and that between two modes of the same substance. Of the former we have an example in this, that we can clearly apprehend substance apart from the mode which we say differs from it; while, on the other hand, we cannot conceive this mode without conceiving the substance itself. There is, for example, a modal distinction between figure or motion and corporeal substance in which both exist; there is a similar distinction between affirmation or recollection and the mind. Of the latter kind we have an illustration in our ability to recognise the one of two modes apart from the other, as figure apart from motion, and motion apart from figure; though we cannot think of either the one or the other without thinking of the common substance in which they adhere. If, for example, a stone is moved, and is withal square, we can, indeed, conceive its square figure without its motion, and reciprocally its motion without its square figure; but we can conceive neither this motion nor this figure apart from the substance of the stone. As for the distinction according to which the mode of one substance is different from another substance, or from the mode of another substance, as the motion of one body is different from another body or from the mind, or as motion is different from doubt, it seems to me that it should be called real rather than modal, because these modes cannot be clearly conceived apart from the really distinct substances of which they are the modes.

LXII. Of the distinction of reason (logical distinction).

Finally, the distinction of reason is that between a substance and some one of its attributes, without which it is impossible, however, we can have a distinct conception of the substance itself; or between two such attributes of a common substance, the one of which we essay to think without the other. This distinction is manifest from our inability to form a clear and distinct idea of such substance, if we separate from it such attribute; or to have a clear perception of the one of two such attributes if we separate it from the other. For example, because any substance which ceases to endure ceases also to exist, duration is not distinct from substance except in thought (RATIONE); and in general all the modes of thinking which we consider as in objects differ only in thought, as well from the objects of which they are thought as from each other in a common object.[Footnote: "and generally all the attributes that lead us to entertain different thoughts of the same thing, such as, for example, the extension of body and its property of divisibility, do not differ from the body which is to us the object of them, or from each other, unless as we sometimes confusedly think the one without thinking the other."—FRENCH.] It occurs, indeed, to me that I have elsewhere classed this kind of distinction with the modal (viz., towards the end of the Reply to the First Objections to the Meditations on the First Philosophy); but there it was only necessary to treat of these distinctions generally, and it was sufficient for my purpose at that time simply to distinguish both of them from the real.

LXIII. How thought and extension may be distinctly known, as constituting, the one the nature of mind, the other that of body.

Thought and extension may be regarded as constituting the natures of intelligent and corporeal substance; and then they must not be otherwise conceived than as the thinking and extended substances themselves, that is, as mind and body, which in this way are conceived with the greatest clearness and distinctness. Moreover, we more easily conceive extended or thinking substance than substance by itself, or with the omission of its thinking or extension. For there is some difficulty in abstracting the notion of substance from the notions of thinking and extension, which, in truth, are only diverse in thought itself (i.e., logically different); and a concept is not more distinct because it comprehends fewer properties, but because we accurately distinguish what is comprehended in it from all other notions.

LXIV. How these may likewise be distinctly conceived as modes of substance.

Thought and extension may be also considered as modes of substance; in as far, namely, as the same mind may have many different thoughts, and the same body, with its size unchanged, may be extended in several diverse ways, at one time more in length and less in breadth or depth, and at another time more in breadth and less in length; and then they are modally distinguished from substance, and can be conceived not less clearly and distinctly, provided they be not regarded as substances or things separated from others, but simply as modes of things. For by regarding them as in the substances of which they are the modes, we distinguish them from these substances, and take them for what in truth they are: whereas, on the other hand, if we wish to consider them apart from the substances in which they are, we should by this itself regard them as self-subsisting things, and thus confound the ideas of mode and substance.

LXV. How we may likewise know their modes.

In the same way we will best apprehend the diverse modes of thought, as intellection, imagination, recollection, volition, etc., and also the diverse modes of extension, or those that belong to extension, as all figures, the situation of parts and their motions, provided we consider them simply as modes of the things in which they are; and motion as far as it is concerned, provided we think merely of locomotion, without seeking to know the force that produces it, and which nevertheless I will essay to explain in its own place.

LXVI. How our sensations, affections, and appetites may be clearly known, although we are frequently wrong in our judgments regarding them.

There remain our sensations, affections, and appetites, of which we may also have a clear knowledge, if we take care to comprehend in the judgments we form of them only that which is precisely contained in our perception of them, and of which we are immediately conscious. There is, however, great difficulty in observing this, at least in respect of sensations; because we have all, without exception, from our youth judged that all the things we perceived by our senses had an existence beyond our thought, and that they were entirely similar to the sensations, that is, perceptions, we ad of them. Thus when, for example, we saw a certain colour, we thought we saw something occupying a place out of us, and which was entirely similar to that idea of colour we were then conscious of; and from the habit of judging in this way, we seemed to see this so clearly and distinctly that we esteemed it (i.e., the externality of the colour) certain and indubitable.

LXVII. That we are frequently deceived in our judgments regarding pain itself.

The same prejudice has place in all our other sensations, even in those of titillation and pain. For though we are not in the habit of believing that there exist out of us objects that resemble titillation and pain, we do not nevertheless consider these sensations as in the mind alone, or in our perception, but as in the hand, or foot, or some other part of our body. There is no reason, however, to constrain us to believe that the pain, for example, which we feel, as it were, in the foot is something out of the mind existing in the foot, or that the light which we see, as it were, in the sun exists in the sun as it is in us. Both these beliefs are prejudices of our early years, as will clearly appear in the sequel.

LXVIII. How in these things what we clearly conceive is to be distinguished from that in which we may be deceived.

But that we may distinguish what is clear in our sensations from what is obscure, we ought most carefully to observe that we possess a clear and distinct knowledge of pain, colour, and other things of this sort, when we consider them simply as sensations or thoughts; but that, when they are judged to be certain things subsisting beyond our mind, we are wholly unable to form any conception of them. Indeed, when any one tells us that he sees colour in a body or feels pain in one of his limbs, this is exactly the same as if he said that he there saw or felt something of the nature of which he was entirely ignorant, or that he did not know what he saw or felt. For although, when less attentively examining his thoughts, a person may easily persuade himself that he has some knowledge of it, since he supposes that there is something resembling that sensation of colour or of pain of which he is conscious; yet, if he reflects on what the sensation of colour or pain represents to him as existing in a coloured body or in a wounded member, he will find that of such he has absolutely no knowledge.

LXIX. That magnitude, figure, etc., are known far differently from colour, pain, etc.

What we have said above will be more manifest; especially if we consider that size in the body perceived, figure, motion (at least local, for philosophers by fancying other kinds of motion have rendered its nature less intelligible to themselves), the situation of parts, duration, number, and those other properties which, as we have already said, we clearly perceive in all bodies, are known by us in a way altogether different from that in which we know what colour is in the same body, or pain, smell, taste, or any other of those properties which I have said above must be referred to the senses. For although when we see a body we are not less assured of its existence from its appearing figured than from its appearing coloured,[Footnote: "by the colour we perceive on occasion of it."— FRENCH.] we yet know with far greater clearness its property of figure than its colour.

LXX. *That we may judge of sensible things in two ways, by the one of which we avoid error, by the other fall into it.*

It is thus manifest that to say we perceive colours in objects is in reality equivalent to saying we perceive something in objects and are yet ignorant of what it is, except as that which determines in us a certain highly vivid and clear sensation, which we call the sensation of colours. There is, however, very great diversity in the manner of judging: for so long as we simply judge that there is an unknown something in objects (that is, in things such as they are, from which the sensation reached us), so far are we from falling into error that, on the contrary, we thus rather provide against it, for we are less apt to judge rashly of a thing which we observe we do not know. But when we think we perceive colours in objects, although we are in reality ignorant of what we then denominate colour, and are unable to conceive any resemblance between the colour we suppose to be in objects, and that of which we are conscious in sensation, yet because we do not observe this, or because there are in objects several properties, as size, figure, number, etc., which, as we clearly know, exist, or may exist in them as they are perceived by our senses or conceived by our understanding, we easily glide into the error of holding that what is called colour in objects is something entirely resembling the colour we perceive, and thereafter of supposing that we have a clear perception of what is in no way perceived by us.

LXXI. *That the chief cause of our errors is to be found in the prejudices of our childhood.*

And here we may notice the first and chief cause of our errors. In early life the mind was so closely bound to the body that it attended to nothing beyond the thoughts by which it perceived the objects that made impression on the body; nor as yet did it refer these thoughts to anything existing beyond itself, but simply felt pain when the body was hurt, or pleasure when anything beneficial to the body occurred, or if the body was so highly affected that it was neither greatly benefited nor hurt, the mind experienced the sensations we call tastes, smells, sounds, heat, cold, light, colours, and the like, which in truth are representative of nothing existing out of our mind, and which vary according to the diversities of the parts and modes in which the body is affected. [Footnote: "which vary according to the diversities of the movements that pass from all parts of our body to the part of the brain to which it (the mind) is closely joined and united."—FRENCH.] The mind at the same time also perceived magnitudes, figures, motions, and the like, which were not presented to it as sensations but as things or the modes of things existing, or at least capable of existing out of thought, although it did not yet observe this difference between these two kinds of perceptions. And afterwards when the machine of the body, which has been so fabricated by nature that it can of its own inherent power move itself in various ways, by turning itself at random on every side, followed after what was useful and avoided what was detrimental; the mind, which was closely connected with it, reflecting on the objects it pursued or avoided, remarked, for the first time, that they existed out of itself, and not only attributed to them magnitudes, figures, motions, and the like, which it apprehended either as things or as the modes of things, but, in addition, attributed to them tastes, odours, and the other ideas of that sort, the sensations of which were caused by itself; [Footnote: "which it perceived on occasion of them" (i.e., of external objects).—FRENCH.] and as it only considered other objects in so far as they were useful to the body, in which it was immersed, it judged that there was greater or less reality in each object, according as the impressions it caused on the body were more or less powerful. Hence arose the belief that there was more substance or body in rocks and metals than in air or water, because the mind perceived in them more hardness and weight. Moreover, the air was thought to be merely nothing so long as we experienced no agitation of it by the wind, or did not feel it hot or cold. And because the stars gave hardly more light than the slender flames of candles, we supposed that each star was but of this size. Again, since the mind did not observe that the earth moved on its axis, or that its superficies was curved like that of a globe, it was on that account more ready to judge the earth immovable and its surface flat. And our mind has been imbued from our infancy with a thousand other prejudices of the same sort which afterwards in our youth we forgot we had accepted without sufficient examination, and admitted as possessed of the highest truth and clearness, as if they had been known by means of our senses, or implanted in us by nature.

LXXII. That the second cause of our errors is that we cannot forget these prejudices.

And although now in our mature years, when the mind, being no longer wholly subject to the body, is not in the habit of referring all things to it, but also seeks to discover the truth of things considered in themselves, we observe the falsehood of a great many of the judgments we had before formed; yet we experience a difficulty in expunging them from our memory, and, so long as they remain there, they give rise to various errors. Thus, for example, since from our earliest years we imagined the stars to be of very small size, we find it highly difficult to rid ourselves of this imagination, although assured by plain astronomical reasons that they are of the greatest,—so prevailing is the power of preconceived opinion.

LXXIII. The third cause is, that we become fatigued by attending to those objects which are not present to the senses; and that we are thus accustomed to judge of these not from present perception but from pre-conceived opinion.

Besides, our mind cannot attend to any object without at length experiencing some pain and fatigue; and of all objects it has the greatest difficulty in attending to those which are present neither to the senses nor to the imagination: whether for the reason that this is natural to it from its union with the body, or because in our early years, being occupied merely with perceptions and imaginations, it has become more familiar with, and acquired greater facility in thinking in those modes than in any other. Hence it also happens that many are unable to conceive any substance except what is imaginable and corporeal, and even sensible. For they are ignorant of the circumstance, that those objects alone are imaginable which consist in extension, motion, and figure, while there are many others besides these that are intelligible; and they persuade themselves that nothing can subsist but body, and, finally, that there is no body which is not sensible. And since in truth we perceive no object such as it is by sense alone [but only by our reason exercised upon sensible objects], as will hereafter be clearly shown, it thus happens that the majority during life perceive nothing unless in a confused way.

LXXIV. The fourth source of our errors is, that we attach our thoughts to words which do not express them with accuracy.

Finally, since for the use of speech we attach all our conceptions to words by which to express them, and commit to memory our thoughts in connection with these terms, and as we afterwards find it more easy to recall the words than the things signified by them, we can scarcely conceive anything with such distinctness as to separate entirely what we conceive from the words that were selected to express it. On this account the majority attend to words rather than to things; and thus very frequently assent to terms without attaching to them any meaning, either because they think they once understood them, or imagine they received them from others by whom they were correctly understood. This, however, is not the place to treat of this matter in detail, seeing the nature of the human body has not yet been expounded, nor the existence even of body established; enough, nevertheless, appears to have been said to enable one to distinguish such of our conceptions as are clear and distinct from those that are obscure and confused.

LXXV. Summary of what must be observed in order to philosophize correctly.

Wherefore if we would philosophize in earnest, and give ourselves to the search after all the truths we are capable of knowing, we must, in the first place, lay aside our prejudices; in other words, we must take care scrupulously to withhold our assent from the opinions we have formerly admitted, until upon new examination we discover that they are true. We must, in the next place, make an orderly review of the notions we have in our minds, and hold as true all and only those which we will clearly and distinctly apprehend. In this way we will observe, first of all, that we exist in so far as it is our nature to think, and at the same time that there is a God upon whom we depend; and after considering his attributes we will be able to investigate the truth of all other things, since God is the cause of them. Besides the notions we have of God and of our mind, we will likewise find that we possess the knowledge of many propositions which are eternally true, as, for example, that nothing cannot be the cause of anything, etc. We will farther discover in our minds the knowledge of a corporeal or extended nature that may be moved, divided, etc., and also of certain sensations that affect us, as of pain, colours, tastes, etc., although we do not yet know the cause of our being so affected; and, comparing what we have now learne'd, by examining those things in their order, with our former confused knowledge of them, we will acquire the habit of forming clear and distinct conceptions of all the objects we are capable of knowing. In these few precepts seem to me to be comprised the most general and important principles of human knowledge.

LXXVI. That we ought to prefer the Divine authority to our perception; [Footnote: "reasonings."—FRENCH]. but that, apart from things revealed, we ought to assent to nothing that we do not clearly apprehend.

Above all, we must impress on our memory the infallible rule, that what God has revealed is incomparably more certain than anything else; and that, we ought to submit our belief to the Divine authority rather than to our own judgment, even although perhaps the light of reason should, with the greatest clearness and evidence, appear to suggest to us something contrary to what is revealed. But in things regarding which there is no revelation, it is by no means consistent with the character of a philosopher to accept as true what he has not ascertained to be such, and to trust more to the senses, in other words, to the inconsiderate judgments of childhood than to the dictates of mature reason.

PART II.

OF THE PRINCIPLES OF MATERIAL THINGS.

I. The grounds on which the existence of material things may be known with certainty.

Although we are all sufficiently persuaded of the existence of material things, yet, since this was before called in question by us, and since we reckoned the persuasion of their existence as among the prejudices of our childhood, it is now necessary for us to investigate the grounds on which this truth may be known with certainty. In the first place, then, it cannot be doubted that every perception we have comes to us from some object different from our mind; for it is not in our power to cause ourselves to experience one perception rather than another, the perception being entirely dependent on the object which affects our senses. It may, indeed, be matter of inquiry whether that object be God, or something different from God; but because we perceive, or rather, stimulated by sense, clearly and distinctly apprehend, certain matter extended in length, breadth, and thickness, the various parts of which have different figures and motions, and give rise to the sensation we have of colours, smells, pain, etc., God would, without question, deserve to be regarded as a deceiver, if he directly and of himself presented to our mind the idea of this extended matter, or merely caused it to be presented to us by some object which possessed neither extension, figure, nor motion. For we clearly conceive this matter as entirely distinct from God, and from ourselves, or our mind; and appear even clearly to discern that the idea of it is formed in us on occasion of objects existing out of our minds, to which it is in every respect similar. But since God cannot deceive us, for this is repugnant to his nature, as has been already remarked, we must unhesitatingly conclude that there exists a certain object extended in length, breadth, and thickness, and possessing all those properties which we clearly apprehend to belong to what is extended. And this extended substance is what we call body or matter.

II. How we likewise know that the human body is closely connected with the mind.

We ought also to conclude that a certain body is more closely united to our mind than any other, because we clearly observe that pain and other sensations affect us without our foreseeing them; and these, the mind is conscious, do not arise from itself alone, nor pertain to it, in so far as it is a thing which thinks, but only in so far as it is united to another thing extended and movable, which is called the human body. But this is not the place to treat in detail of this matter.

III. That the perceptions of the senses do not teach us what is in reality in things, but what is beneficial of hurtful to the composite whole of mind and body.

It will be sufficient to remark that the perceptions of the senses are merely to be referred to this intimate union of the human body and mind, and that they usually make us aware of what, in external objects, may be useful or adverse to this union, but do not present to us these objects as they are in themselves, unless occasionally and by accident. For, after this observation, we will without difficulty lay aside the prejudices of the senses, and will have recourse to our understanding alone on this question by reflecting carefully on the ideas implanted in it by nature.

IV. That the nature of body consists not in weight hardness, colour and the like, but in extension alone.

In this way we will discern that the nature of matter or body, considered in general, does not consist in its being hard, or ponderous, or coloured, or that which affects our senses in any other way, but simply in its being a substance extended in length, breadth, and depth. For with respect to hardness, we know nothing of it by sense farther than that the parts of hard bodies resist the motion of our hands on coming into contact with them; but if every time our hands moved towards any part, all the bodies in that place receded as quickly as our hands approached, we should never feel hardness; and yet we have no reason to believe that bodies which might thus recede would on this account lose that which makes them bodies. The nature of body does not, therefore, consist in hardness. In the same way, it may be shown that weight, colour, and all the other qualities of this sort, which are perceived in corporeal matter, may be taken from it, itself meanwhile remaining entire: it thus follows that the nature of body depends on none of these.

V. That the truth regarding the nature of body is obscured by the opinions respecting rarefaction and a vacuum with which we are pre- occupied.

There still remain two causes to prevent its being fully admitted that the true nature of body consists in extension alone. The first is the prevalent opinion, that most bodies admit of being so rarefied and condensed that, when rarefied, they have greater extension than when condensed; and some even have subtilized to such a degree as to make a distinction between the substance of body and its quantity, and between quantity itself and extension. The second cause is this, that where we conceive only extension in length, breadth, and depth, we are not in the habit of saying that body is there, but only space and further void space, which the generality believe to be a mere negation.

VI. In what way rarefaction takes place.

But with regard to rarefaction and condensation, whoever gives his attention to his own thoughts, and admits nothing of which he is not clearly conscious, will not suppose that there is anything in those processes further than a change of figure in the body rarefied or condensed: so that, in other words, rare bodies are those between the parts of which there are numerous distances filled with other bodies; and dense bodies, on the other hand, those whose parts approaching each other, either diminish these distances or take them wholly away, in the latter of which cases the body is rendered absolutely dense. The body, however, when condensed, has not, therefore, less extension than when the parts embrace a greater space, owing to their removal from each other, and their dispersion into branches. For we ought not to attribute to it the extension of the pores or distances which its parts do not occupy when it is rarefied, but to the other bodies that fill these interstices; just as when we see a sponge full of water or any other liquid, we do not suppose that each part of the sponge has on this account greater extension than when compressed and dry, but only that its pores are wider, and therefore that the body is diffused over a larger space.

VII. That rarefaction cannot be intelligibly explained unless in the way here proposed.

And indeed I am unable to discover the force of the reasons which have induced some to say that rarefaction is the result of the augmentation of the quantity of body, rather than to explain it on the principle exemplified in the case of a sponge. For although when air or water is rarefied we do not see any of the pores that are rendered large, or the new body that is added to occupy them, it is yet less agreeable to reason to suppose something that is unintelligible for the purpose of giving a verbal and merely apparent explanation of the rarefaction of bodies, than to conclude, because of their rarefaction, that there are pores or distances between the parts which are increased in size, and filled with some new body. Nor ought we to refrain from assenting to this explanation, because we perceive this new body by none of our senses, for there is no reason which obliges us to believe that we should perceive by our senses all the bodies in existence. And we see that it is very easy to explain rarefaction in this manner, but impossible in any other; for, in fine, there would be, as appears to me, a manifest contradiction in supposing that any body was increased by a quantity or extension which it had not before, without the addition to it of a new extended substance, in other words, of another body, because it is impossible to conceive any addition of extension or quantity to a thing without supposing the addition of a substance having quantity or extension, as will more clearly appear from what follows.

VIII. That quantity and number differ only in thought (RATIONE) from that which has quantity and is numbered.

For quantity differs from extended substance, and number from what is numbered, not in reality but merely in our thought; so that, for example, we may consider the whole nature of a corporeal substance which is comprised in a space of ten feet, although we do not attend to this measure of ten feet, for the obvious reason that the thing conceived is of the same nature in any part of that space as in the whole; and, on the other hand, we can conceive the number ten, as also a continuous quantity of ten feet, without thinking of this determinate substance, because the concept of the number ten is manifestly the same whether we consider a number of ten feet or ten of anything else; and we can conceive a continuous quantity of ten feet without thinking of this or that determinate substance, although we cannot conceive it without some extended substance of which it is the quantity. It is in reality, however, impossible that any, even the least part, of such quantity or extension, can be taken away, without the retrenchment at the same time of as much of the substance, nor, on the other hand, can we lessen the substance, without at the same time taking as much from the quantity or extension.

IX. That corporeal substance, when distinguished from its quantity, is confusedly conceived as something incorporeal.

Although perhaps some express themselves otherwise on this matter, I am nevertheless convinced that they do not think differently from what I have now said: for when they distinguish (corporeal) substance from extension or quantity, they either mean nothing by the word (corporeal) substance, or they form in their minds merely a confused idea of incorporeal substance, which they falsely attribute to corporeal, and leave to extension the true idea of this corporeal substance; which extension they call an accident, but with such impropriety as to make it easy to discover that their words are not in harmony with their thoughts.

X. What space or internal place is.

Space or internal place, and the corporeal substance which is comprised in it, are not different in reality, but merely in the mode in which they are wont to be conceived by us. For, in truth, the same extension in length, breadth, and depth, which constitutes space, constitutes body; and the difference between them lies only in this, that in body we consider extension as particular, and conceive it to change with the body; whereas in space we attribute to extension a generic unity, so that after taking from a certain space the body which occupied it, we do not suppose that we have at the same time removed the extension of the space, because it appears to us that the same extension remains there so long as it is of the same magnitude and figure, and preserves the same situation in respect to certain bodies around it, by means of which we determine this space.

XI. How space is not in reality different from corporeal substance.

And indeed it will be easy to discern that it is the same extension which constitutes the nature of body as of space, and that these two things are mutually diverse only as the nature of the genus and species differs from that of the individual, provided we reflect on the idea we have of any body, taking a stone for example, and reject all that is not essential to the nature of body. In the first place, then, hardness may be rejected, because if the stone were liquefied or reduced to powder, it would no longer possess hardness, and yet would not cease to be a body; colour also may be thrown out of account, because we have frequently seen stones so transparent as to have no colour; again, we may reject weight, because we have the case of fire, which, though very light, is still a body; and, finally, we may reject cold, heat, and all the other qualities of this sort, either because they are not considered as in the stone, or because, with the change of these qualities, the stone is not supposed to have lost the nature of body. After this examination we will find that nothing remains in the idea of body, except that it is something extended in length, breadth, and depth; and this something is comprised in our idea of space, not only of that which is full of body, but even of what is called void space.

XII. How space differs from body in our mode of conceiving it.

There is, however, some difference between them in the mode of conception; for if we remove a stone from the space or place in which it was, we conceive that its extension also is taken away, because we regard this as particular, and inseparable from the stone itself: but meanwhile we suppose that the same extension of place in which this stone was remains, although the place of the stone be occupied by wood, water, air, or by any other body, or be even supposed vacant, because we now consider extension in general, and think that the same is common to stones, wood, water, air, and other bodies, and even to a vacuum itself, if there is any such thing, provided it be of the same magnitude and figure as before, and preserve the same situation among the external bodies which determine this space.

XIII. What external place is.

The reason of which is, that the words place and space signify nothing really different from body which is said to be in place, but merely designate its magnitude, figure, and situation among other bodies. For it is necessary, in order to determine this situation, to regard certain other bodies which we consider as immovable; and, according as we look to different bodies, we may see that the same thing at the same time does and does not change place. For example, when a vessel is being carried out to sea, a person sitting at the stern may be said to remain always in one place, if we look to the parts of the vessel, since with respect to these he preserves the same situation; and on the other hand, if regard be had to the neighbouring shores, the same person will seem to be perpetually changing place, seeing he is constantly receding from one shore and approaching another. And besides, if we suppose that the earth moves, and that it makes precisely as much way from west to east as the vessel from east to west, we will again say that the person at the stern does not change his place, because this place will be determined by certain immovable points which we imagine to be in the heavens. But if at length we are persuaded that there are no points really immovable in the universe, as will hereafter be shown to be probable, we will thence conclude that nothing has a permanent place unless in so far as it is fixed by our thought.

XIV. Wherein place and space differ.

The terms place and space, however, differ in signification, because place more expressly designates situation than magnitude or figure, while, on the other hand, we think of the latter when we speak of space. For we frequently say that a thing succeeds to the place of another, although it be not exactly of the same magnitude or figure; but we do not therefore admit that it occupies the same space as the other; and when the situation is changed we say that the place also is changed, although there are the same magnitude and figure as before: so that when we say that a thing is in a particular place, we mean merely that it is situated in a determinate way in respect of certain other objects; and when we add that it occupies such a space or place, we understand besides that it is of such determinate magnitude and figure as exactly to fill this space.

XV. How external place is rightly taken for the superficies of the surrounding body.

And thus we never indeed distinguish space from extension in length, breadth, and depth; we sometimes, however, consider place as in the thing placed, and at other times as out of it. Internal place indeed differs in no way from space; but external place may be taken for the superficies that immediately surrounds the thing placed. It ought to be remarked that by superficies we do not here understand any part of the surrounding body, but only the boundary between the surrounding and surrounded bodies, which is nothing more than a mode; or at least that we speak of superficies in general which is no part of one body rather than another, but is always considered the same, provided it retain the same magnitude and figure. For although the whole surrounding body with its superficies were changed, it would not be supposed that the body which was surrounded by it had therefore changed its place, if it meanwhile preserved the same situation with respect to the other bodies that are regarded as immovable. Thus, if we suppose that a boat is carried in one direction by the current of a stream, and impelled by the wind in the opposite with an equal force, so that its situation with respect to the banks is not changed, we will readily admit that it remains in the same place, although the whole superficies which surrounds it is incessantly changing.

XVI. That a vacuum or space in which there is absolutely no body is repugnant to reason.

With regard to a vacuum, in the philosophical sense of the term, that is, a space in which there is no substance, it is evident that such does not exist, seeing the extension of space or internal place is not different from that of body. For since from this alone, that a body has extension in length, breadth, and depth, we have reason to conclude that it is a substance, it being absolutely contradictory that nothing should possess extension, we ought to form a similar inference regarding the space which is supposed void, viz., that since there is extension in it there is necessarily also substance.

XVII. That a vacuum in the ordinary use of the term does not exclude all body.

And, in truth, by the term vacuum in its common use, we do not mean a place or space in which there is absolutely nothing, but only a place in which there is none of those things we presume ought to be there. Thus, because a pitcher is made to hold water, it is said to be empty when it is merely filled with air; or if there are no fish in a fish-pond, we say there is nothing in it, although it be full of water; thus a vessel is said to be empty, when, in place of the merchandise which it was designed to carry, it is loaded with sand only, to enable it to resist the violence of the wind; and, finally, it is in the same sense that we say space is void when it contains nothing sensible, although it contain created and self-subsisting matter; for we are not in the habit of considering the bodies near us, unless in so far as they cause in our organs of sense, impressions strong enough to enable us to perceive them. And if, in place of keeping in mind what ought to be understood by these terms a vacuum and nothing, we afterwards suppose that in the space we called a vacuum, there is not only no sensible object, but no object at all, we will fall into the same error as if, because a pitcher in which there is nothing but air, is, in common speech, said to be empty, we were therefore to judge that the air contained in it is not a substance (RES SUBSISTENS).

XVIII. How the prejudice of an absolute vacuum is to be corrected.

We have almost all fallen into this error from the earliest age, for, observing that there is no necessary connection between a vessel and the body it contains, we thought that God at least could take from a vessel the body which occupied it, without it being necessary that any other should be put in the place of the one removed. But that we may be able now to correct this false opinion, it is necessary to remark that there is in truth no connection between the vessel and the particular body which it contains, but that there is an absolutely necessary connection between the concave figure of the vessel and the extension considered generally which must be comprised in this cavity; so that it is not more contradictory to conceive a mountain without a valley than such a cavity without the extension it contains, or this extension apart from an extended substance, for, as we have often said, of nothing there can be no extension. And accordingly, if it be asked what would happen were God to remove from a vessel all the body contained in it, without permitting another body to occupy its place, the answer must be that the sides of the vessel would thus come into proximity with each other. For two bodies must touch each other when there is nothing between them, and it is manifestly contradictory for two bodies to be apart, in other words, that there should be a distance between them, and this distance yet be nothing; for all distance is a mode of extension, and cannot therefore exist without an extended substance.

XIX. That this confirms what was said of rarefaction.

After we have thus remarked that the nature of corporeal substance consists only in its being an extended thing, and that its extension is not different from that which we attribute to space, however empty, it is easy to discover the impossibility of any one of its parts in any way whatsoever occupying more space at one time than at another, and thus of being otherwise rarefied than in the way explained above; and it is easy to perceive also that there cannot be more matter or body in a vessel when it is filled with lead or gold, or any other body however heavy and hard, than when it but contains air and is supposed to be empty: for the quantity of the parts of which a body is composed does not depend on their weight or hardness, but only on the extension, which is always equal in the same vase.

XX. That from this the non-existence of atoms may likewise be demonstrated.

We likewise discover that there cannot exist any atoms or parts of matter that are of their own nature indivisible. For however small we suppose these parts to be, yet because they are necessarily extended, we are always able in thought to divide any one of them into two or more smaller parts, and may accordingly admit their divisibility. For there is nothing we can divide in thought which we do not thereby recognize to be divisible; and, therefore, were we to judge it indivisible our judgment would not be in harmony with the knowledge we have of the thing; and although we should even suppose that God had reduced any particle of matter to a smallness so extreme that it did not admit of being further divided, it would nevertheless be improperly styled indivisible, for though God had rendered the particle so small that it was not in the power of any creature to divide it, he could not however deprive himself of the ability to do so, since it is absolutely impossible for him to lessen his own omnipotence, as was before observed. Wherefore, absolutely speaking, the smallest extended particle is always divisible, since it is such of its very nature.

XXI. It is thus also demonstrated that the extension of the world is indefinite.

We further discover that this world or the whole (universitas) of corporeal substance, is extended without limit, for wherever we fix a limit, we still not only imagine beyond it spaces indefinitely extended, but perceive these to be truly imaginable, in other words, to be in reality such as we imagine them; so that they contain in them corporeal substance indefinitely extended, for, as has been already shown at length, the idea of extension which we conceive in any space whatever is plainly identical with the idea of corporeal substance.

XXII. It also follows that the matter of the heavens and earth is the same, and that there cannot be a plurality of worlds.

And it may also be easily inferred from all this that the earth and heavens are made of the same matter; and that even although there were an infinity of worlds, they would all be composed of this matter; from which it follows that a plurality of worlds is impossible, because we clearly conceive that the matter whose nature consists only in its being an extended substance, already wholly occupies all the imaginable spaces where these other worlds could alone be, and we cannot find in ourselves the idea of any other matter.

XXIII. That all the variety of matter, or the diversity of its forms, depends on motion.

There is therefore but one kind of matter in the whole universe, and this we know only by its being extended. All the properties we distinctly perceive to belong to it are reducible to its capacity of being divided and moved according to its parts; and accordingly it is capable of all those affections which we perceive can arise from the motion of its parts. For the partition of matter in thought makes no change in it; but all variation of it, or diversity of form, depends on motion. The philosophers even seem universally to have observed this, for they said that nature was the principle of motion and rest, and by nature they understood that by which all corporeal things become such as they are found in experience.

XXIV. What motion is, taking the term in its common use.

But motion (viz., local, for I can conceive no other kind of motion, and therefore I do not think we ought to suppose there is any other in nature), in the ordinary sense of the term, is nothing more than the action by which a body passes from one place to another. And just as we have remarked above that the same thing may be said to change and not to change place at the same time, so also we may say that the same thing is at the same time moved and not moved. Thus, for example, a person seated in a vessel which is setting sail, thinks he is in motion if he look to the shore that he has left, and consider it as fixed; but not if he regard the ship itself, among the parts of which he preserves always the same situation. Moreover, because we are accustomed to suppose that there is no motion without action, and that in rest there is the cessation of action, the person thus seated is more properly said to be at rest than in motion, seeing he is not conscious of being in action.

XXV. What motion is properly so called.

But if, instead of occupying ourselves with that which has no foundation, unless in ordinary usage, we desire to know what ought to be understood by motion according to the truth of the thing, we may say, in order to give it a determinate nature, that it is THE TRANSPORTING OF ONE PART OF MATTER OR OF ONE BODY FROM THE VICINITY OF THOSE BODIES THAT ARE IN IMMEDIATE CONTACT WITH IT, OR WHICH WE REGARD AS AT REST, to the vicinity of other bodies. By a body as a part of matter, I understand all that which is transferred together, although it be perhaps composed of several parts, which in themselves have other motions; and I say that it is the transporting and not the force or action which transports, with the view of showing that motion is always in the movable thing, not in that which moves; for it seems to me that we are not accustomed to distinguish these two things with sufficient accuracy. Farther, I understand that it is a mode of the movable thing, and not a substance, just as figure is a property of the thing figured, and repose of that which is at rest.

PART III.

OF THE VISIBLE WORLD.

I. That we cannot think too highly of the works of God.

Having now ascertained certain principles of material things, which were sought, not by the prejudices of the senses, but by the light of reason, and which thus possess so great evidence that we cannot doubt of their truth, it remains for us to consider whether from these alone we can deduce the explication of all the phenomena of nature. We will commence with those phenomena that are of the greatest generality, and upon which the others depend, as, for example, with the general structure of this whole visible world. But in order to our philosophizing aright regarding this, two things are first of all to be observed. The first is, that we should ever bear in mind the infinity of the power and goodness of God, that we may not fear falling into error by imagining his works to be too great, beautiful, and perfect, but that we may, on the contrary, take care lest, by supposing limits to them of which we have no certain knowledge, we appear to think less highly than we ought of the power of God.

II. That we ought to beware lest, in our presumption, we imagine that the ends which God proposed to himself in the creation of the world are understood by us.

The second is, that we should beware of presuming too highly of ourselves, as it seems we should do if we supposed certain limits to the world, without being assured of their existence either by natural reasons or by divine revelation, as if the power of our thought extended beyond what God has in reality made; but likewise still more if we persuaded ourselves that all things were created by God for us only, or if we merely supposed that we could comprehend by the power of our intellect the ends which God proposed to himself in creating the universe.

III. In what sense it may be said that all things were created for the sake of man.

For although, as far as regards morals, it may be a pious thought to believe that God made all things for us, seeing we may thus be incited to greater gratitude and love toward him; and although it is even in some sense true, because there is no created thing of which we cannot make some use, if it be only that of exercising our mind in considering it, and honouring God on account of it, it is yet by no means probable that all things were created for us in this way that God had no other end in their creation; and this supposition would be plainly ridiculous and inept in physical reasoning, for we do not doubt but that many things exist, or formerly existed and have now ceased to be, which were never seen or known by man, and were never of use to him.

PART IV.

OF THE EARTH.

CLXXXVIII. *Of what is to be borrowed from disquisitions on animals and man to advance the knowledge of material objects.*

I should add nothing farther to this the Fourth Part of the Principles of Philosophy, did I purpose carrying out my original design of writing a Fifth and Sixth Part, the one treating of things possessed of life, that is, animals and plants, and the other of man. But because I have not yet acquired sufficient knowledge of all the matters of which I should desire to treat in these two last parts, and do not know whether I shall ever have sufficient leisure to finish them, I will here subjoin a few things regarding the objects of our senses, that I may not, for the sake of the latter, delay too long the publication of the former parts, or of what may be desiderated in them, which I might have reserved for explanation in those others: for I have hitherto described this earth, and generally the whole visible world, as if it were merely a machine in which there was nothing at all to consider except the figures and motions of its parts, whereas our senses present to us many other things, for example colours, smells, sounds, and the like, of which, if I did not speak at all, it would be thought I had omitted the explication of the majority of the objects that are in nature.

CLXXXIX. *What perception (SENSUS) is, and how we perceive.*

We must know, therefore, that although the human soul is united to the whole body, it has, nevertheless, its principal seat in the brain, where alone it not only understands and imagines, but also perceives; and this by the medium of the nerves, which are extended like threads from the brain to all the other members, with which they are so connected that we can hardly touch any one of them without moving the extremities of some of the nerves spread over it; and this motion passes to the other extremities of those nerves which are collected in the brain round the seat of the soul, [Footnote: *** FOOTNOTE NOT VISIBLE IN PAGE IMAGE (#98, Text p 195)] as I have already explained with sufficient minuteness in the fourth chapter of the Dioptrics. But the movements which are thus excited in the brain by the nerves variously affect the soul or mind, which is intimately conjoined with the brain, according to the diversity of the motions themselves. And the diverse affections of the mind or thoughts that immediately arise from these motions, are called perceptions of the senses (SENSUUM PERCEPTIONES), or, as we commonly speak, sensations (SENSUS).

CXC. Of the distinction of the senses; and, first, of the internal, that is, of the affections of the mind (passions), and the natural appetites.

The varieties of these sensations depend, firstly, on the diversity of the nerves themselves, and, secondly, of the movements that are made in each nerve. We have not, however, as many different senses as there are nerves. We can distinguish but seven principal classes of nerves, of which two belong to the internal, and the other five to the external senses. The nerves which extend to the stomach, the oesophagus, the fauces, and the other internal parts that are subservient to our natural wants, constitute one of our internal senses. This is called the natural appetite (APPETITUS NATURALIS). The other internal sense, which embraces all the emotions (COMMOTIONES) of the mind or passions, and affections, as joy, sadness, love, hate, and the like, depends upon the nerves which extend to the heart and the parts about the heart, and are exceedingly small; for, by way of example, when the blood happens to be pure and well tempered, so that it dilates in the heart more readily and strongly than usual, this so enlarges and moves the small nerves scattered around the orifices, that there is thence a corresponding movement in the brain, which affects the mind with a certain natural feeling of joy; and as often as these same nerves are moved in the same way, although this is by other causes, they excite in our mind the same feeling (sensus, sentiment). Thus, the imagination of the enjoyment of a good does not contain in itself the feeling of joy, but it causes the animal spirits to pass from the brain to the muscles in which these nerves are inserted; and thus dilating the orifices of the heart, it also causes these small nerves to move in the way appointed by nature to afford the sensation of joy. Thus, when we receive news, the mind first of all judges of it, and if the news be good, it rejoices with that intellectual joy (GAUDIUM INTELLECTUALE) which is independent of any emotion (COMMOTIO) of the body, and which the Stoics did not deny to their wise man [although they supposed him exempt from all passion]. But as soon as this joy passes from the understanding to the imagination, the spirits flow from the brain to the muscles that are about the heart, and there excite the motion of the small nerves, by means of which another motion is caused in the brain, which affects the mind with the sensation of animal joy (LAETITIA ANIMALIS). On the same principle, when the blood is so thick that it flows but sparingly into the ventricles of the heart, and is not there sufficiently dilated, it excites in the same nerves a motion quite different from the preceding, which, communicated to the brain, gives to the mind the sensation of sadness, although the mind itself is perhaps ignorant of the cause of its sadness. And all the other causes which move these nerves in the same way may also give to the mind the same sensation. But the other movements of the same nerves produce other effects, as the feelings of love, hate, fear, anger, etc., as far as they are merely affections or passions of the mind; in other words, as far as they are confused thoughts which the mind has not from itself alone, but from its being closely joined to the body, from which it receives impressions; for there is the widest difference between these passions and the distinct thoughts which we have of what ought to be loved, or chosen, or shunned, etc., [although these are often enough found together]. The natural appetites, as hunger, thirst, and the others, are likewise sensations excited in the mind by means of the nerves of the stomach, fauces, and other parts, and are entirely different from the will which we have to eat, drink, [and to do all that which we think proper for the conservation of our body]; but, because this will or appetition almost always accompanies them, they are therefore named appetites.

CXCI. Of the external senses; and first of touch.

We commonly reckon the external senses five in number, because there are as many different kinds of objects which move the nerves and their organs, and an equal number of kinds of confused thoughts excited in the soul by these emotions. In the first place, the nerves terminating in the skin of the whole body can be touched through this medium by any terrene objects whatever, and moved by these wholes, in one way by their hardness, in another by their gravity, in a third by their heat, in a fourth by their humidity, etc.—and in as many diverse modes as they are either moved or hindered from their ordinary motion, to that extent are diverse sensations excited in the mind, from which a corresponding number of tactile qualities derive their appellations. Besides this, when these nerves are moved a little more powerfully than usual, but not nevertheless to the degree by which our body is in any way hurt, there thus arises a sensation of titillation, which is naturally agreeable to the mind, because it testifies to it of the powers of the body with which it is joined, [in that the latter can suffer the action causing this titillation, without being hurt]. But if this action be strong enough to hurt our body in any way, this gives to our mind the sensation of pain. And we thus see why corporeal pleasure and pain, although sensations of quite an opposite character, arise nevertheless from causes nearly alike.

CXCII. Of taste.

In the second place, the other nerves scattered over the tongue and the parts in its vicinity are diversely moved by the particles of the same bodies, separated from each other and floating in the saliva in the mouth, and thus cause sensations of diverse tastes according to the diversity of figure in these particles. [Footnote: In the French this section begins, "Taste, after touch the grossest of the senses," etc.]

CXCIII. Of smell.

Thirdly, two nerves also or appendages of the brain, for they do not go beyond the limits of the skull, are moved by the particles of terrestrial bodies, separated and flying in the air, not indeed by all particles indifferently, but by those only that are sufficiently subtle and penetrating to enter the pores of the bone we call the spongy, when drawn into the nostrils, and thus to reach the nerves. From the different motions of these particles arise the sensations of the different smells.

CXCIV. Of hearing.

Fourthly, there are two nerves within the ears, so attached to three small bones that are mutually sustaining, and the first of which rests on the small membrane that covers the cavity we call the tympanum of the ear, that all the diverse vibrations which the surrounding air communicates to this membrane are transmitted to the mind by these nerves, and these vibrations give rise, according to their diversity, to the sensations of the different sounds.

CXCV. Of sight.

Finally, the extremities of the optic nerves, composing the coat in the eyes called the retina, are not moved by the air nor by any terrestrial object, but only by the globules of the second element, whence we have the sense of light and colours: as I have already at sufficient length explained in the Dioptrics and treatise of Meteors. [Footnote: In the French this section begins, "Finally, sight is the most subtle of all the senses," etc.]

CXCVI. That the soul perceives only in so far as it is in the brain.

It is clearly established, however, that the soul does not perceive in so far as it is in each member of the body, but only in so far as it is in the brain, where the nerves by their movements convey to it the diverse actions of the external objects that touch the parts of the body in which they are inserted. For, in the first place, there are various maladies, which, though they affect the brain alone, yet bring disorder upon, or deprive us altogether of the use of, our senses, just as sleep, which affects the brain only, and yet takes from us daily during a great part of our time the faculty of perception, which afterwards in our waking state is restored to us. The second proof is, that though there be no disease in the brain, [or in the members in which the organs of the external senses are], it is nevertheless sufficient to take away sensation from the part of the body where the nerves terminate, if only the movement of one of the nerves that extend from the brain to these members be obstructed in any part of the distance that is between the two. And the last proof is, that we sometimes feel pain as if in certain of our members, the cause of which, however, is not in these members where it is felt, but somewhere nearer the brain, through which the nerves pass that give to the mind the sensation of it. I could establish this fact by innumerable experiments; I will here, however, merely refer to one of them. A girl suffering from a bad ulcer in the hand, had her eyes bandaged whenever the surgeon came to visit her, not being able to bear the sight of the dressing of the sore; and, the gangrene having spread, after the expiry of a few days the arm was amputated from the elbow [without the girl's knowledge]; linen cloths tied one above the other were substituted in place of the part amputated, so that she remained for some time without knowing that the operation had been performed, and meanwhile she complained of feeling various pains, sometimes in one finger of the hand that was cut off, and sometimes in another. The only explanation of this is, that the nerves which before stretched downwards from the brain to the hand, and then terminated in the arm close to the elbow, were there moved in the same way as they required to be moved before in the hand for the purpose of impressing on the mind residing in the brain the sensation of pain in this or that finger. [And this clearly shows that the pain of the hand is not felt by the mind in so far as it is in the hand, but in so far as it is in the brain.]

CXCVII. That the nature of the mind is such that from the motion alone of body the various sensations can be excited in it.

In the next place, it can be proved that our mind is of such a nature that the motions of the body alone are sufficient to excite in it all sorts of thoughts, without it being necessary that these should in any way resemble the motions which give rise to them, and especially that these motions can excite in it those confused thoughts called sensations (SENSUS, SENSATIONES). For we see that words, whether uttered by the voice or merely written, excite in our minds all kinds of thoughts and emotions. On the same paper, with the same pen and ink, by merely moving the point of the pen over the paper in a particular way, we can trace letters that will raise in the minds of our readers the thoughts of combats, tempests, or the furies, and the passions of indignation and sorrow; in place of which, if the pen be moved in another way hardly different from the former, this slight change will cause thoughts widely different from the above, such as those of repose, peace, pleasantness, and the quite opposite passions of love and joy. Some one will perhaps object that writing and speech do not immediately excite in the mind any passions, or imaginations of things different from the letters and sounds, but afford simply the knowledge of these, on occasion of which the mind, understanding the signification of the words, afterwards excites in itself the imaginations and passions that correspond to the words. But what will be said of the sensations of pain and titillation? The motion merely of a sword cutting a part of our skin causes pain, [but does not on that account make us aware of the motion or figure of the sword]. And it is certain that this sensation of pain is not less different from the motion that causes it, or from that of the part of our body which the sword cuts, than are the sensations we have of colour, sound, odour, or taste. On this ground we may conclude that our mind is of such a nature that the motions alone of certain bodies can also easily excite in it all the other sensations, as the motion of a sword excites in it the sensation of pain.

CXCVIII. *That by our senses we know nothing of external objects beyond their figure [or situation], magnitude, and motion.*

Besides, we observe no such difference between the nerves as to lead us to judge that one set of them convey to the brain from the organs of the external senses anything different from another, or that anything at all reaches the brain besides the local motion of the nerves themselves. And we see that local motion alone causes in us not only the sensation of titillation and of pain, but also of light and sounds. For if we receive a blow on the eye of sufficient force to cause the vibration of the stroke to reach the retina, we see numerous sparks of fire, which, nevertheless, are not out of our eye; and when we stop our ear with our finger, we hear a humming sound, the cause of which can only proceed from the agitation of the air that is shut up within it. Finally, we frequently observe that heat [hardness, weight], and the other sensible qualities, as far as they are in objects, and also the forms of those bodies that are purely material, as, for example, the forms of fire, are produced in them by the motion of certain other bodies, and that these in their turn likewise produce other motions in other bodies. And we can easily conceive how the motion of one body may be caused by that of another, and diversified by the size, figure, and situation of its parts, but we are wholly unable to conceive how these same things (viz., size, figure, and motion), can produce something else of a nature entirely different from themselves, as, for example, those substantial forms and real qualities which many philosophers suppose to be in bodies; nor likewise can we conceive how these qualities or forms possess force to cause motions in other bodies. But since we know, from the nature of our soul, that the diverse motions of body are sufficient to produce in it all the sensations which it has, and since we learn from experience that several of its sensations are in reality caused by such motions, while we do not discover that anything besides these motions ever passes from the organs of the external senses to the brain, we have reason to conclude that we in no way likewise apprehend that in external objects, which we call light, colour, smell, taste, sound, heat or cold, and the other tactile qualities, or that which we call their substantial forms, unless as the various dispositions of these objects which have the power of moving our nerves in various ways. [Footnote: "the diverse figures, situations, magnitudes, and motions of their parts."—French.]

CXCIX. *That there is no phenomenon of nature whose explanation has been omitted in this treatise.*

And thus it may be gathered, from an enumeration that is easily made, that there is no phenomenon of nature whose explanation has been omitted in this treatise; for beyond what is perceived by the senses, there is nothing that can be considered a phenomenon of nature. But leaving out of account motion, magnitude, figure, [and the situation of the parts of each body], which I have explained as they exist in body, we perceive nothing out of us by our senses except light, colours, smells, tastes, sounds, and the tactile qualities; and these I have recently shown to be nothing more, at least so far as they are known to us, than certain dispositions of the objects, consisting in magnitude, figure, and motion.

CC. *That this treatise contains no principles which are not universally received; and that this philosophy is not new, but of all others the most ancient and common.*

But I am desirous also that it should be observed that, though I have here endeavoured to give an explanation of the whole nature of material things, I have nevertheless made use of no principle which was not received and approved by Aristotle, and by the other philosophers of all ages; so that this philosophy, so far from being new, is of all others the most ancient and common: for I have in truth merely considered the figure, motion, and magnitude of bodies, and examined what must follow from their mutual concourse on the principles of mechanics, which are confirmed by certain and daily experience. But no one ever doubted that bodies are moved, and that they are of various sizes and figures, according to the diversity of which their motions also vary, and that from mutual collision those somewhat greater than others are divided into many smaller, and thus change figure. We have experience of the truth of this, not merely by a single sense, but by several, as touch, sight, and hearing: we also distinctly imagine and understand it. This cannot be said of any of the other things that fall under our senses, as colours, sounds, and the like; for each of these affects but one of our senses, and merely impresses upon our imagination a confused image of itself, affording our understanding no distinct knowledge of what it is.

CCI. *That sensible bodies are composed of insensible particles.*

But I allow many particles in each body that are perceived by none of our senses, and this will not perhaps be approved of by those who take the senses for the measure of the knowable. [We greatly wrong human reason, however, as appears to me, if we suppose that it does not go beyond the eye-sight]; for no one can doubt that there are bodies so small as not to be perceptible by any of our senses, provided he only consider what is each moment added to those bodies that are being increased little by little, and what is taken from those that are diminished in the same way. A tree increases daily, and it is impossible to conceive how it becomes greater than it was before, unless we at the same time conceive that some body is added to it. But who ever observed by the senses those small bodies that are in one day added to a tree while growing? Among the philosophers at least, those who hold that quantity is indefinitely divisible, ought to admit that in the division the parts may become so small as to be wholly imperceptible. And indeed it ought not to be a matter of surprise, that we are unable to perceive very minute bodies; for the nerves that must be moved by objects to cause perception are not themselves very minute, but are like small cords, being composed of a quantity of smaller fibres, and thus the most minute bodies are not capable of moving them. Nor do I think that any one who makes use of his reason will deny that we philosophize with much greater truth when we judge of what takes place in those small bodies which are imperceptible from their minuteness only, after the analogy of what we see occurring in those we do perceive, [and in this way explain all that is in nature, as I have essayed to do in this treatise], than when we give an explanation of the same things by inventing I know not what novelties, that have no relation to the things we actually perceive, [as first matter, substantial forms, and all that grand array of qualities which many are in the habit of supposing, each of which is more difficult to comprehend than all that is professed to be explained by means of them].

CCII. That the philosophy of Democritus is not less different from ours than from the common. [Footnote: "that of Aristotle or the others."—French.]

But it may be said that Democritus also supposed certain corpuscles that were of various figures, sizes, and motions, from the heaping together and mutual concourse of which all sensible bodies arose; and, nevertheless, his mode of philosophizing is commonly rejected by all. To this I reply that the philosophy of Democritus was never rejected by any one, because he allowed the existence of bodies smaller than those we perceive, and attributed to them diverse sizes, figures, and motions, for no one can doubt that there are in reality such, as we have already shown; but it was rejected, in the first place, because he supposed that these corpuscles were indivisible, on which ground I also reject it; in the second place, because he imagined there was a vacuum about them, which I show to be impossible; thirdly, because he attributed gravity to these bodies, of which I deny the existence in any body, in so far as a body is considered by itself, because it is a quality that depends on the relations of situation and motion which several bodies bear to each other; and, finally, because he has not explained in particular how all things arose from the concourse of corpuscles alone, or, if he gave this explanation with regard to a few of them, his whole reasoning was far from being coherent, [or such as would warrant us in extending the same explanation to the whole of nature]. This, at least, is the verdict we must give regarding his philosophy, if we may judge of his opinions from what has been handed down to us in writing. I leave it to others to determine whether the philosophy I profess possesses a valid coherency, [and whether on its principles we can make the requisite number of deductions; and, inasmuch as the consideration of figure, magnitude, and motion has been admitted by Aristotle and by all the others, as well as by Democritus, and since I reject all that the latter has supposed, with this single exception, while I reject generally all that has been supposed by the others, it is plain that this mode of philosophizing has no more affinity with that of Democritus than of any other particular sect].

CCIII. *How we may arrive at the knowledge of the figures, [magnitudes], and motions of the insensible particles of bodies.*

But, since I assign determinate figures, magnitudes, and motions to the insensible particles of bodies, as if I had seen them, whereas I admit that they do not fall under the senses, some one will perhaps demand how I have come by my knowledge of them. [To this I reply, that I first considered in general all the clear and distinct notions of material things that are to be found in our understanding, and that, finding no others except those of figures, magnitudes, and motions, and of the rules according to which these three things can be diversified by each other, which rules are the principles of geometry and mechanics, I judged that all the knowledge man can have of nature must of necessity be drawn from this source; because all the other notions we have of sensible things, as confused and obscure, can be of no avail in affording us the knowledge of anything out of ourselves, but must serve rather to impede it]. Thereupon, taking as my ground of inference the simplest and best known of the principles that have been implanted in our minds by nature, I considered the chief differences that could possibly subsist between the magnitudes, and figures, and situations of bodies insensible on account of their smallness alone, and what sensible effects could be produced by their various modes of coming into contact; and afterwards, when I found like effects in the bodies that we perceive by our senses, I judged that they could have been thus produced, especially since no other mode of explaining them could be devised. And in this matter the example of several bodies made by art was of great service to me: for I recognize no difference between these and natural bodies beyond this, that the effects of machines depend for the most part on the agency of certain instruments, which, as they must bear some proportion to the hands of those who make them, are always so large that their figures and motions can be seen; in place of which, the effects of natural bodies almost always depend upon certain organs so minute as to escape our senses. And it is certain that all the rules of mechanics belong also to physics, of which it is a part or species, [so that all that is artificial is withal natural]: for it is not less natural for a clock, made of the requisite number of wheels, to mark the hours, than for a tree, which has sprung from this or that seed, to produce the fruit peculiar to it. Accordingly, just as those who are familiar with automata, when they are informed of the use of a machine, and see some of its parts, easily infer from these the way in which the others, that are not seen by them, are made; so from considering the sensible effects and parts of natural bodies, I have essayed to determine the character of their causes and insensible parts.

CCIV. *That, touching the things which our senses do not perceive, it is sufficient to explain how they can be,* [*and that this is all that Aristotle has essayed*].

But here some one will perhaps reply, that although I have supposed causes which could produce all natural objects, we ought not on this account to conclude that they were produced by these causes; for, just as the same artisan can make two clocks, which, though they both equally well indicate the time, and are not different in outward appearance, have nevertheless nothing resembling in the composition of their wheels; so doubtless the Supreme Maker of things has an infinity of diverse means at his disposal, by each of which he could have made all the things of this world to appear as we see them, without it being possible for the human mind to know which of all these means he chose to employ. I most freely concede this; and I believe that I have done all that was required, if the causes I have assigned are such that their effects accurately correspond to all the phenomena of nature, without determining whether it is by these or by others that they are actually produced. And it will be sufficient for the use of life to know the causes thus imagined, for medicine, mechanics, and in general all the arts to which the knowledge of physics is of service, have for their end only those effects that are sensible, and that are accordingly to be reckoned among the phenomena of nature. [Footnote: "have for their end only to apply certain sensible bodies to each other in such a way that, in the course of natural causes, certain sensible effects may be produced; and we will be able to accomplish this quite as well by considering the series of certain causes thus imagined, although false, as if they were the true, since this series is supposed similar as far as regards sensible effects."-French.]

And lest it should be supposed that Aristotle did, or professed to do, anything more than this, it ought to be remembered that he himself expressly says, at the commencement of the seventh chapter of the first book of the Meteorologies, that, with regard to things which are not manifest to the senses, he thinks to adduce sufficient reasons and demonstrations of them, if he only shows that they may be such as he explains them. [Footnote: words in Greek]

CCV. That nevertheless there is a moral certainty that all the things of this world are such as has been here shown they may be.

But nevertheless, that I may not wrong the truth by supposing it less certain than it is, I will here distinguish two kinds of certitude. The first is called moral, that is, a certainty sufficient for the conduct of life, though, if we look to the absolute power of God, what is morally certain may be false. [Thus, those who never visited Rome do not doubt that it is a city of Italy, though it might be that all from whom they got their information were deceived]. Again, if any one, wishing to decipher a letter written in Latin characters that are not placed in regular order, bethinks himself of reading a B wherever an A is found, and a C wherever there is a B, and thus of substituting in place of each letter the one which follows it in the order of the alphabet, and if by this means he finds that there are certain Latin words composed of these, he will not doubt that the true meaning of the writing is contained in these words, although he may discover this only by conjecture, and although it is possible that the writer of it did not arrange the letters on this principle of alphabetical order, but on some other, and thus concealed another meaning in it: for this is so improbable [especially when the cipher contains a number of words] as to seem incredible. But they who observe how many things regarding the magnet, fire, and the fabric of the whole world, are here deduced from a very small number of principles, though they deemed that I had taken them up at random and without grounds, will yet perhaps acknowledge that it could hardly happen that so many things should cohere if these principles were false.

CCVI. That we possess even more than a moral certainty of it.

Besides, there are some, even among natural, things which we judge to be absolutely certain. [Absolute certainty arises when we judge that it is impossible a thing can be otherwise than as we think it]. This certainty is founded on the metaphysical ground, that, as God is supremely good and the source of all truth, the faculty of distinguishing truth from error which he gave us, cannot be fallacious so long as we use it aright, and distinctly perceive anything by it. Of this character are the demonstrations of mathematics, the knowledge that material things exist, and the clear reasonings that are formed regarding them. The results I have given in this treatise will perhaps be admitted to a place in the class of truths that are absolutely certain, if it be considered that they are deduced in a continuous series from the first and most elementary principles of human knowledge; especially if it be sufficiently understood that we can perceive no external objects unless some local motion be caused by them in our nerves, and that such motion cannot be caused by the fixed stars, owing to their great distance from us, unless a motion be also produced in them and in the whole heavens lying between them and us: for these points being admitted, all the others, at least the more general doctrines which I have advanced regarding the world or earth [e. g., the fluidity of the heavens, Part III., Section XLVI.], will appear to be almost the only possible explanations of the phenomena they present.

CCVII. That, however, I submit all my opinions to the authority of the church.

Nevertheless, lest I should presume too far, I affirm nothing, but submit all these my opinions to the authority of the church and the judgment of the more sage; and I desire no one to believe anything I may have said, unless he is constrained to admit it by the force and evidence of reason.

www.ingramcontent.com/pod-product-compliance
Lightning Source LLC
Chambersburg PA
CBHW071154160426
43196CB00011B/2080